Buying a Franchise in Canada:

Understanding and Negotiating Your Franchise Agreement

Tony Wilson, BA (Hons.), LLB

Self-Counsel Press
(a division of)
International Self-Counsel Press Ltd.
Canada   USA

Self-Counsel Press acknowledges the financial support of the Government of Canada through the Book Publishing Industry Development Program (BPIDP) for our publishing activities.

Printed in Canada.

First edition: 2005

Second edition: 2009

Library and Archives Canada Cataloguing in Publication

Wilson, Tony

    Buying a franchise in Canada / Tony Wilson. -- 2nd ed.

ISBN 978-1-55180-847-5

    1. Franchises (Retail trade)--Canada. I. Title.

HF5429.235.C3W57 2009   658.8'7080971   C2009-902220-6

FSC — Mixed Sources
Product group from well-managed forests, and other controlled sources
www.fsc.org Cert no. SW-COC-002358
© 1996 Forest Stewardship Council

Self-Counsel Press
(a division of)
International Self-Counsel Press Ltd.

1481 Charlotte Road
North Vancouver, BC V7J 1H1
Canada

1704 N. State Street
Bellingham, WA 98225
USA

CONTENTS

ACKNOWLEDGEMENTS

I am greatly indebted to my friend and mentor, Len Polsky, for his suggestions, advice, edits, and very helpful contributions to the various and numerous versions of the original paper that became still another paper that then became part of this book. Some of these contributions, I'm happy to say, still remain embedded here and there notwithstanding the fact that over time, the original paper was modified, edited, added to, subtracted from, melded, moulded, sliced, diced, paraphrased, and amended numerous times and in a dozen ways.

I would also like to thank my friend and colleague, James Bond, who looked over a final proof of this book before it went to print, pointing out minor gaffes and major flaws.

Both Len's and James' contributions have made this book into something far better than what I could have done on my own, although any glitches and gaffes that still remain must be attributed to me alone.

Finally, I must thank my wife Mary-Jane, who is chiefly responsible for setting the events in motion that led to this book even being written in the first place, and for putting up with me spending hours on a computer to finish it.

NOTICE

FOREWORD

There are books out there about franchising for people seeking to buy a franchise. The problem is, most of them are American and deal with US concepts that are not necessarily relevant to Canada and the way franchising operates in this country. The Canadian legal books that I am aware of are excellent, but deal with franchising from the perspective of the *franchisor*. These books are instructive if you are the one starting the franchise, but not as helpful if you are the franchisee seeking to buy the franchise. As well, most of them are for lawyers.

There was nothing that I was aware of (when I started this book) that was written to assist franchisees in making the single biggest investment of their lives. This book was written to help those people understand some of the legal issues prospective franchisees must be aware of before they acquire a franchised business. The first edition of this book sold over 4,000 copies and I continue to receive emails from Canadians thanking me for writing it and helping them to understand the pros and cons of becoming a franchisee in Canada.

Little has changed since the first edition; there have been some terminology changes in the United States (UFOC to FDD). PEI has adopted legislation pertaining to franchising, as has New Brunswick (although at the time of writing, that province has yet to approve regulations dealing with disclosure obligations).

Some provinces have legislation that regulates franchising, but the other provinces and territories do not. In these provinces, franchisees must be more careful before they venture into the world of franchising because there is little but the common law to protect them.

Hopefully, this book will help explain the pros and cons of buying a franchise in Canada.

INTRODUCTION

Around 1995, I was asked to write a paper for Continuing Legal Education (CLE) in British Columbia on legal issues relating to franchise law. As I recall, the program was called Advising Small Businesses and it was geared to assist general lawyers who might need specialized information on legal areas they might not see very often in general practice. Different lawyers were asked to write papers from their areas of specialty such as trade-marks, corporate tax, estate planning, and, if memory serves me, there may have been one on entertainment law as well.

The program was designed to give the general lawyer a starting point on areas of law he or she might not have day-to-day experience with, which would enable him or her to get up to speed in that area and competently advise the client (or failing that, call the author for the real answer).

I was asked to cover franchise law because franchising was perceived to be a boutique legal area that the organizers thought was important for the general practitioner to know something about. After all, a franchise agreement is one of those things that lands on a lawyer's desk from time to time. It would help if the lawyer knew how to deal with it (or failing that, who to refer the client to).

The fact that I was asked to write a paper on franchise law was not unusual. Since 1988, franchise law has been the largest part of my legal practice, and by 1995, I had written numerous franchising-related articles for magazines, legal publications, CLE, and newspapers across Canada. I still do. I also regularly speak about franchise law at franchising conventions, trade shows, and at least one law school, and have recently served as the legal advisor to the Canadian Franchise Association in British Columbia.

Until 1995, most of my writing had been geared to the needs of the franchisor. I would write or lecture about "Starting a franchise," "Expanding a franchise," "How to make more money out of your franchisees," or "How to enforce your franchise agreement against a franchisee."

Like most books and articles on franchising in Canada, my writing and speaking were targeted to the needs of what I call the "head office" types — the corporate executives from Toronto or Vancouver or the United States who own or manage the Tim Hortons', McDonald's, and Jiffy Lubes of this world. These head-office types or "franchisors" tended to pay their lawyers lots of money to draft the franchise agreements, subleases, security agreements, and other contracts that govern the franchise relationship.

Around the same time, it occurred to me that nothing I had written had ever been geared to the small-business person who actually bought the franchise rights; the one who took the risk and borrowed money against the family house; the one who invested the severance package into the actual "store" where you get your donuts; the husband and wife who buy the franchised business, pay its debts, pay the employees before they pay themselves, pay the rent, order and count the inventory, cut a cheque for the royalties, and answer to the franchisor when things don't go well. To my knowledge, there was little or nothing of a legal nature for the people who reap the rewards if the venture succeeds but who lose their shirts (and perhaps their houses) if the venture fails.

In fact, what written material that was out there in Canada (when compared to the United States) mainly assisted franchisors and their lawyers, enabling them to "draft around" or otherwise deal with particularly unhelpful court decisions. In short, I discovered that there was very little written legal material to guide prospective franchisees in making one of the most important business decisions of their lives.

As the lawyers who would be reading my original CLE paper were not likely to be representing the franchisors, I decided to write my original CLE paper from the perspective of the franchisee. It was delivered to an audience of lawyers, and I thought, more or less forgotten over the years. However, around 1999, I met a Victoria lawyer who, when he heard my name, immediately said to me, "When a franchise agreement hits my desk, I go to your CLE paper right away. I use it as a checklist. It's the Bible."

As compliments from one's colleagues at the bar are difficult to come by on the best of days, comparing something I had written to the Bible was among the better forms of kudos I'd ever received from another lawyer.

Over time, the original paper was modified, edited, added to, subtracted from, melded, moulded, sliced, diced, paraphrased, and amended numerous times and in a dozen ways.

I always thought that it would be useful to expand the original paper into a full-length book for prospective franchisees to refer to in their hour and a half of need. The idea was to add a sample franchise agreement with commentary on the various sections of the agreement so that readers could see what a section meant, why it was there, and if it was worth arguing about. I decided to do this for Self-Counsel Press, and approached the publisher on, of all things, a cruise ship. That, then, is how this book came to be. Many readers from all across Canada who read the first edition of this book contacted me with their legal concerns. The second edition will, I hope, help future franchisees understand their agreements, and I welcome all comments.

This book will address some of the legal issues that you should be aware of if you are considering "buying" into a franchise. I will try to address the following type of questions:

- Is the initial franchise fee too high for the industry?

- Is the royalty rate within the going rate for the industry?

- What parts of the agreement are negotiable and what parts are not?

- How protected is the "protected" territory?

- Is an "exclusive" territory really exclusive?

- What about sales over the Internet or by mail order?

- Should you or your lawyer spend time negotiating a restrictive covenant or does that suggest to the franchisor that you are not a team player and may be a future problem within the system?

- Is the advertising fund going to be spent predominantly on advertisements in media far away from your franchise where it may not assist your franchise in obtaining customers?

- How can you discover the status of the franchisor's trade-marks?

- Will you or the franchisor control the lease for the franchised location?

- Will you or the franchisor be responsible for arranging the construction and development of the franchised location?

- What is the personal guarantee and can it be avoided or capped in any way?

- Should the deposit monies under a deposit agreement be held in a lawyer's trust account until the agreement is concluded?

- Is the franchisor receiving any tenant inducement money from the landlord for signing the head lease, and should the franchisor be entitled to retain any of it for its own account?

- When should you agree to the governing law clause even if it's not the law of your province?

- Does the franchisor need to give a portion of rebates from suppliers to you?

- How easy will it be for you to resell or renew the franchised business?

- What happens when there's a US form of the franchise agreement that contains provisions totally inapplicable to business in Canada?

- Will the franchisor have a right of approval (and other conditions that must be met?)

- Will the franchisor have a right to buy the franchised business itself?

- What are the franchisor's conditions for renewing the agreement?

- What is the effect of the *Alberta Franchises Act* and the *Ontario Arthur Wishart Act* (Franchise Disclosure), 2000, on franchising both inside and outside those provinces? What about other provinces with laws covering franchising?

These are the types of practical questions that you and your lawyer must deal with on a regular basis. The answers are both legal and business related. I try to answer them in this book to give you a sense of what is normal and accepted in franchising from the perspective of the franchise agreement and franchise law. That said, readers should note my comments come from the legal side and not the business or accounting side. Other materials written by accountants and other business professionals may assist the reader in the same way that I hope to have done from the legal side. In addition, I do not deal with the laws of Quebec, the Quebec Civil Code, or the uniqueness of the Quebec market in any way. My comments pertain to the common-law provinces only, although some of my observations may apply to Quebec in the most general way.

A few words about that mysterious word "negotiation." First, in my experience, franchisors rarely, if ever, admit to negotiating their agreements, but they will, if pressed, admit to "clarifying" them or "discussing" them as the circumstances warrant. So if you are dealing with a franchisor without a lawyer, characterize your "negotiations" as "discussions" or "clarifications." Avoid the "n" word. "N" can stand for "no" as much as it can stand for "negotiation." ("C" stands for both "clever" and "clarification.") Spin is everywhere these days. You have to live with it, and spin your words to deal with the circumstances.

Secondly, in my experience, attempting to negotiate, quibble, and nitpick the normal, expected, and standard clauses in a franchise agreement (and even the not so normal ones) may lose the prospective franchisee (and his or her lawyer) a great deal of credibility with the franchisor and its lawyer. The prospective franchisee (and again, his or her lawyer) may not be taken as seriously by the franchisor — especially an established one with a successful concept, a well-respected brand, and many locations — and could well be marginalized to some extent by the franchisor, whose attitude may be accurately reflected as follows: "This is standard in all franchise agreements. Who is this idiot?"

Mind you, if you're dealing with a start-up franchisor needy of making a sale, with few or no franchised units, a questionable concept, an iffy location, a trade-mark that is pending, or other factors that strike you as unusual or above the usual level of risk you're prepared to take, then by all means, discuss and clarify your heart out, and live by the maxim, "If you don't ask, you don't get." The franchisor can always say, "This is standard in all franchise agreements. Who is this idiot?" But perhaps the franchisor won't. You just might find you have more of an edge in these circumstances.

In Part 1 of this book, I discuss the issues surrounding what franchising is and who you are dealing with when buying into a franchise, as well as the topic of master franchising.

In Part 2, I provide a sample franchise agreement similar to the type I've prepared for franchisor clients. I've created a hypothetical franchisor and business model (Internet café and donuts), and I've put some deliberate errors and omissions in the agreement to illustrate mistakes or errors franchisors or their lawyers can make.

The sample franchise agreement is broken down into sections, and below each section there is an explanation. The explanations discuss the sorts of legal and business issues that I would raise if I were reviewing the franchise agreement for a prospective franchisee. I also explain when something is normal and when it may be best left alone, no matter how much the prospective franchisee doesn't like the clause. Again, if there are factors that strike you as unusual or above the usual level of risk, pick five or six of the best points to negotiate and don't fiddle so much with the boilerplate. Concentrate, if possible, on the money issues; the deal points. (Know how to hold them and when to fold them!)

Also, know what is unenforceable and what is best left alone (lest you turn something that is unenforceable into something that is enforceable ... but against you). I raise some of these issues in the book, but a franchise lawyer is probably a better guide to the terms of your specific agreement.

In Part 3, I discuss the disclosure document. Alberta, Prince Edward Island, and Ontario have franchise legislation that requires the preparation and delivery of a disclosure document that represents all material facts about the franchise to franchisees prior to the signing of the franchise agreement. (In the case of Ontario, this document must be presented prior to signing any agreement relating to the franchise and accepting any deposit money from a franchisee.) New Brunswick has passed legislation similar to that of the other provinces that have regulated franchising, but regulations were not yet in place at the time of this edition. Law reform commissions from other provinces (such as Manitoba) have looked at the issue, and within a decade I expect legislation to be the norm across Canada.

Part 3 is by no means a legal treatise on disclosure documents. The point is to show you what one might look like so you can look at the one you receive and say, "Oh, that's why they put that in here!" The Canadian Franchise Association also requires its members to provide similar disclosure documents. Part 3 includes a sample Alberta/Ontario joint disclosure document with explanations similar to what I have done with the franchise agreement in Part 2. I have also strategically placed errors in this document to illustrate mistakes franchisors might make, frighten away copiers, and to otherwise make a point.

As a final note, you wouldn't give yourself a root canal, would you? You would go to the dentist. That being said, this book is not a substitute for using a lawyer. So even though you might not see the need to use one, I encourage you to hire a lawyer with some experience in franchise law to assist you in all stages of the franchise transaction. Franchise law is a specialty area, and few lawyers have experience in this area.

The Canadian Franchise Association (CFA) is the only national association of franchise systems and service providers in the franchise industry in Canada. They will be able to refer you to a number of experienced franchise lawyers who can provide you with competent advice on acquiring your franchised business or the remedies which may be available to you if things go wrong. The CFA's headquarters are in Toronto, Ontario, and the office can be reached by telephone at 1-800-665-4232 (or you can find out information from their website at www.cfa.ca.)

I also encourage you to hire an accountant to assist you with structuring the business and tax planning.

Reading this book and using a lawyer (even a franchise lawyer) is no guarantee that you will get the deal you want from a franchisor, and it's certainly no guarantee that your franchised business will be successful. Success is often a function of many things, including the skills at operating the franchised system and inclination to work hard building the business. (Just because the investment goes sideways does not mean the franchisor is at fault. It may be that you are not the "right franchisee" for this particular franchise or perhaps any franchise at all.)

This book will help you be better informed to make the decision to acquire a franchise. At the very least, it will give you a better understanding of the legal issues surrounding perhaps the single largest business venture in which you might ever be involved. At the very most, it may assist you in spotting problem areas and allow for negotiation of these agreements with the franchisor. Purchasers of this book are invited to contact me for assistance, should the need arise. You can email me at tonywilson1@mac.com or twilson@boughton.ca, or telephone me at 604-684-1800. As I do this for a living, I encourage enquiries from prospective franchisees from across Canada (as long as you appreciate that I do this for a living).

As this book is a general guide, I try to provide general comments and general solutions. I provide anecdotal observations based solely on my own personal experience from years of representing franchisees and just as many years drafting long and complicated franchise agreements for franchisors. When I have to speak about the law or make reference to a statute or legal concept, I will usually do this in my own irreverent and glib style. In doing so, I'll try to provide straightforward and simple answers, rather than more complicated and consequently more precise explanations that might make the *Law Review* somewhere or impress a judge. That's because as a reader of this book, you don't need the *Law Review* and you don't need the latest case law because you aren't negotiating with a judge. Instead, you will need practical common sense and general advice that will assist you in the process and lead you to ask more informed questions of your franchise lawyer and the franchisor itself. Readers of this book, (some of whom may be lawyers), will appreciate the sacrifices to detail and thoroughness that must come with common sense, brevity, and generality.

PART 1
THE BASICS OF FRANCHISING

1

UNDERSTANDING FRANCHISING

1. WHAT IS FRANCHISING?

Franchising, or as we sometimes call it, "business format franchising," can be defined as an ongoing contractual relationship between the franchisor on the one hand and the franchisee on the other. Under the franchise agreement, the franchisor grants the franchisee the licensed right for a period of time to —

- market a product or service;

- use the franchisor's trade-mark and business system; and

- use the franchisor's "know-how" in the operation of the business.

In exchange, the franchisee is required to —

- conform to the franchisor's business system, methods, and procedures;

- maintain the franchisor's quality standards; and

- pay a fee to the franchisor (which is usually an initial franchise fee and a continuing monthly or weekly royalty).

The franchisor is the entity that grants franchise rights to the franchisee. Although a franchise agreement is different than a lease, you might think of it in lease-like terms in which a "landlord" leases space in a building to the "tenant" for a period of time under a "lease." In exchange for this right to use the space, the tenant pays the landlord "rent." When the lease expires or is terminated, the tenant no longer has the right to use the space. During the term of the lease, the tenant must comply with the provisions of the lease and the rules and regulations under it.

Franchising is not entirely similar, but it's similar enough for our purposes. Instead of the franchisor granting you the right to rent space, the franchisor is granting you the right to use its business system and its trade-mark. In exchange, you agree to pay the franchisor a fee — normally an initial franchise fee and an ongoing royalty based upon a percentage of the gross sales generated by your franchised business. In addition to the initial franchise fee and royalties for the use of the franchisor's business system, you must also comply with the franchise agreement and with the franchisor's operating procedures, which is normally set out in its operations manual. Strictly speaking, you don't "buy" the franchise. You acquire the licensed rights to use the franchisor's business system and trade-mark for a period of time. When those licensed rights have expired or are terminated, they revert back to the franchisor. The franchisor can, if it so chooses, license the franchise rights to somebody else.

You can see business format franchising in action virtually everywhere (e.g., restaurants, hotels, real estate companies, travel agencies, convenience stores, printing stores, camera stores, tax preparation outlets, cash advance outlets, muffler shops, fast food outlets, and, believe it or not, law firms). All you have to do is visit your local shopping centre or strip mall to see how prevalent franchising has become. In one form or another, you're surrounded by franchises. In 2004, franchised businesses accounted for the employment of at least 1,000,000 Canadians, so even if you don't particularly like fast food outlets in your local mall, or relish the thought of yet another muffler shop down the road, you must realize that it's a phenomenally important segment of our economy. Our standard of living is in part based on the vibrancy of this industry and its ability to create opportunities, livelihoods, and jobs for others.

It must also be remembered that franchising is, more than anything else, a means of business expansion, using capital obtained from the franchisee to fund expansion. (The cynics among us have an acronym for this. It's called OPM and it stands for Other People's Money.) The franchisor's business is being expanded not only through the franchisee's efforts but also due to direct and indirect contributions of money by the franchisee. It has been said that companies that do not need to franchise (because they have the capital necessary to finance expansion), don't. (Starbucks is an example of one of the companies that don't need to franchise.)

For a hundred different reasons, franchising works well. But it doesn't always work, and it's important for all prospective franchisees to realize that.

2. IS A LICENSE AGREEMENT THE SAME AS A FRANCHISE AGREEMENT?

Sometimes franchisors will deliberately call their contracts "license agreements" instead of franchise agreements. This is largely done for marketing reasons. Franchising is often perceived as the home of fast food and french fries. Calling the contract a "license agreement" may give the agreement and, I suppose, the franchise system an air of panache and sophistication that a franchise might lack in the eyes of mortals. Nevertheless, you should be aware that all franchises are essentially "licenses." A license is the right to use the property of another; it does not convey ownership. Accordingly, if there is a fee such as an initial license fee and/or an ongoing royalty fee, and there is the licensed use of the licensor's trade-mark, and the licensee has been granted the right to engage in the business of offering, selling, or distributing goods or services under a marketing plan or system substantially prescribed by the licensor, then it is a franchise, whatever the licensor calls it.

Ontario, Prince Edward Island, and Alberta have specific legislation governing franchising, which provides definitions of what a "franchise" is, regardless of what the "licensor" has called its business model.

3. A BRIEF HISTORY OF FRANCHISING

Back in the mists of ancient time (when a Quarter Pounder with Cheese® meant nothing and Colonel Sander's parents were still in diapers), it's said that franchising was born. Although some have suggested it started in England with the Crown granting exclusive territories to tax collectors for the collection of the 13th century equivalent of GST, for us in the modern world, common wisdom seems to agree that it started with the Singer Sewing Corporation (sewing machines) in the United States. Singer licensed retail stores to sell their sewing machines and sewing supplies in the 19th century. This evolved over the 20th century, and other businesses adopted the model; chief among them being soft drink bottling companies and gas stations.

For those of you who might recall the 1960s and 1970s as being the salad days of rock and roll, free love, and funny cigarettes, it was also the heyday of franchising. The United States became the grand central station of franchising activity; so much so that franchising became the subject of government legislation and regulation. (Around this time, the Alberta government also got involved with franchising legislation and regulation.)

The government did not get involved in the regulation of franchises because it needed the money, or because it wanted to take over the McDonald's corporation and run it like the US defense department. Although McDonald's and some other well-known brands were working rather nicely, thank you very much, the state legislators got involved because many other concepts were not running as well. Some consumers (in this case, those voters who were acquiring the franchises) lost their shirts (and their houses) as a result of getting into franchises in which the franchisor wasn't capitalized enough, or misrepresentations were made by franchisors or their salespeople to get the consumers into the deal. Complaints were made to politicians and the government reacted.

Laws were enacted that treated the sale of a franchise like a "securities" offering, which required franchisors to make disclosure of material facts to franchisees and to give them some time (i.e., 14 days) to do their due diligence and think about the deal before they signed on. In short, the politicians got involved because a few bad operators caused them to get involved. (Government doesn't tend to get involved unless events force it to or people are pressuring it to.)

4. US DISCLOSURE AGREEMENTS AND REGULATIONS

Since the 1970s, US-based franchisors have been subject to a witches' brew of state and federal laws governing the sale and operation of franchises to franchisees. Currently, US-based franchisors are subject to either the Federal Trade Commission Rule on franchising or a regulatory review in select states. The Federal Trade Commission Rule on franchising requires disclosure of all material facts to prospective franchisees through the use of a disclosure document (sometimes referred to as a Uniform Franchise Offering Circular [UFOC]). This is now called a Franchise Disclosure Document (FDD) in the United States. Franchisors can also be subject to regulatory review in approximately 15 US states that currently have legislation specifically regulating franchisors. As of the date of writing, those states are California, Hawaii, Illinois, Indiana, Maryland, Michigan, Minnesota, New York, North Dakota, Oregon, Rhode Island, South Dakota, Virginia, Washington, and Wisconsin (although some registration requirements differ markedly in these states).

In these registration states, unless the franchisor obtains or otherwise qualifies for an exemption from the authorities, a document similar to a securities prospectus must be prepared by the franchisor's lawyers, and must usually be filed with and approved by the state regulatory authority together with the franchisor's franchise agreement, sublease, trade-mark license agreement, general security agreement, and other agreements that normally comprise the package to be signed by the franchisee.

In most cases, the franchisor's audited or reviewed financial statements must also form part of the disclosure package, which is in and of itself an expensive undertaking. But the state authorities don't just "rubber stamp" a franchisor just because the franchisor has submitted the documentation to the regulators. The state regulatory authorities read and review the material and may reject the franchisor altogether, or impose conditions on the franchisor's ability to trade in franchises in that state. This could mean that the franchisor is required to hold a portion of collected initial franchise fees in escrow for a period of time or it may mean capitalization requirements and other conditions.

As you might appreciate, the preparation of these documents by hordes of well-paid attorneys, the vetting process with state regulatory agencies, and the tangled web of rules under which franchisors are required to lawfully "sell" their franchises is extremely complicated, very specialized, and lawyer intensive. It costs a lot of money to start a franchise in the US. Franchising south of the border is not for the faint of heart or those who live in abject fear of large legal bills.

5. ARE US-BASED FRANCHISORS REQUIRED TO GIVE CANADIAN FRANCHISEES DISCLOSURE DOCUMENTS?

US-based franchisors do not always give and are not always required to give disclosure documents to prospective Canadian franchisees. As a prospective Canadian franchisee, you might not be provided with this information even if you ask for it.

It's possible this material could be on the public record and a great deal of information can be learned about a US-based franchisor from its FDD. Accordingly, if you have been approached by a US-based franchisor, but have not been provided with a copy of its FDD, you should ask for it. If the US franchisor refuses to give you a copy of its FDD (your heightened sense of suspicion having now been justifiably aroused), you might well wonder why, given that it is normally a publicly obtainable document and you can probably get a copy of it from the private company FRANdata (www.frandata.com) or from FranchiseHelp (www.franchisehelp.com).

The following list outlines the types of "material facts" that would be useful for you to know in advance of making your decision to buy into the concept:

- Bankruptcy and previous convictions of principals

- Outstanding litigation against or by franchisees

- Net worth of the franchisor

- Expected range of a franchisee's initial investment costs

- Product and service restrictions

- Number of units that have ceased doing business (i.e., failed) in the previous 12-month period

- Names and addresses of existing franchisees

- What the standard form of franchise agreement looks like

- Other facts that the franchisor's lawyers have deemed to be material and therefore must be disclosed

- Litigation against the franchisor and its directors and officers

A good reason why you might not be given a copy of the disclosure document is because it's irrelevant to you and has little or no bearing on the franchisor with whom you would be contracting, such as in circumstances in which a prospective Canadian franchisee is not contracting directly with the American franchisor (which is subject to US regulation), but with a Canadian subsidiary or master franchisee (which may not be subject to US regulation). In other words, this information could be very valuable to you if you were negotiating and contracting directly with the US-based franchisor that is the subject of the disclosure document.

Quite often, the American-based franchisor has "master franchised" or otherwise licensed its rights to franchise all of Canada (or certain Canadian provinces) to someone else; normally an unrelated Canadian company with different directors, officers, and shareholders than the US franchisor and with a totally different corporate history. (See Chapter 3 for more information on master franchising.) Or perhaps the US franchisor has created a Canadian subsidiary to franchise in Canada, and this subsidiary company is not bound by US laws. In that case, all the information you have obtained on the franchisor isn't quite as helpful as you might have first thought because the franchisor isn't the party you're dealing with.

For information on Canadian disclosure documents, see Part 3 of this book.

6. HAS THE US AGREEMENT BEEN CONVERTED TO A CANADIAN AGREEMENT?

Be mindful of US agreements that have not been Canadianized. A US agreement is relatively easy to spot and not just by the spelling of colour, labour, centre, and neighbour! A US agreement may contain references to the Lanham Act rather than our Canadian *Trade-Marks Act* or it may refer to Chapter 11 instead of our *Bankruptcy and Insolvency Act*.

The US agreement might have "offering circular" provisions in the agreement that don't directly relate to Alberta or Ontario. It may contain terms such as FTC or FDD, which mean little or nothing to us in Canada. You probably won't find a reference to GST or PST either. Measurements might not be expressed metrically. Bilingual packaging and labelling may be totally ignored as well.

The fact that products and equipment may have to be imported from the US into Canada may not have been considered in anyone's pro forma financials, putting the Canadian franchisee at a competitive disadvantage — if not abject hardship — if all the inventory has to come only from one bakery in San Francisco or one factory in Boston. The fact that products imported into Canada may have import duties attached to them, or may not in fact be importable at all, or that such products may require different packaging and labelling than required in the US may have been totally missed by our cousins south of the border (who might not expect to see French on the back of Cornflakes boxes, and all other boxes sold in this country). If that weren't enough, the currency that you'll be paying your royalties with will be US dollars, even though your customers will be paying you with Canadian dollars. So US franchise agreements in which the minor (but important) distinctions between our two nations are not dealt with are cause for concern, especially if you are on the receiving end of such an agreement.

The US agreement will usually choose a US state as the governing law of contact and the place in which all legal proceedings concerning the contract will be heard, rather than a nice city such as Vancouver or even a sensible place such as somewhere within the province in which the franchised business just happens to operate.

In very extreme cases, the franchisor's US lawyers will somehow have forgotten about the border between Canada and the US and will require Canadian-based franchisees and their principals to comply with all sorts of inapplicable US laws including, of all things, the Patriot Act! (Don't laugh; I've seen it done!) Try to avoid entering a contract in which Canadian law and Canadian concepts have not been dealt with. It simply means the franchisor's lawyers failed both history and geography, and suggests that the franchisor doesn't really want to spend the money to convert its US agreement into a Canadian one. If they aren't prepared to spend the money to convert their US agreement to a Canadian one, how do you think they'll be dealing with their Canadian franchisees?

It's possible that a US-based franchisor may not vet its standard US franchise agreement with Canadian counsel before it starts granting franchises in Canada. If the agreement is governed by US law, you may well be bound by some or all of these US laws. If the agreement is governed by the laws of the jurisdiction in which the franchised business is located (e.g., BC), then perhaps the franchisor would have some enforceability problems down the road, as the US concepts that supposedly apply to the agreement have limited or no applicability in Canada. (At the very least, it will make lawyers that deal with conflicts of law happy, content, and wealthy!)

There also seems to be a different style and tone in the usual Canadian form of franchise agreement (when compared to the style and tone of the usual US agreement). Some US-based franchisors have been more than surprised when they have discovered that the ironclad, tough, and controlling form of agreement filled to the gunwales with legal provisions that overprotect the franchisor is regularly and resoundingly rejected in the Canadian franchisee marketplace, as too iron-clad, tough, controlling, and filled to the gunwales with too many provisions that overprotect the franchisor. Canadians are, after all, the only people in the world that say thank you to bank machines; you'd expect our franchise agreements would be polite as well.

What seems to be forgotten in all this is that some of the same legal specialists who might review the US agreement on behalf of the Canadian franchisee may well be the same people who write these agreements on behalf of the Canadian franchisor. (It's a small fraternity after all! In Canada, no more than 50 Canadian lawyers specialize in franchise law at the time of writing this book.)

If you have retained a lawyer with some familiarity with franchising (and my advice is that you should), he or she will know what is normal for the Canadian marketplace. Your franchise lawyer will advise you about what is not normal, what is over-the-top, what is overreaching, and what is just plain wacky (see references to the Patriot Act, above). It may well be that your franchise lawyer may tell you, "This agreement is way out of line and nobody in their right mind should sign it."

In short, if the American franchisor hasn't Canadianized its US form of agreement, you should ask the very sensible question: Why?

7. LABOUR ISSUES

Provincial labour relations boards have looked at franchised retail and restaurant labour issues with great scrutiny. There have been stronger attempts by unions to protect their members' bargaining rights, or to expand these rights to more retail and food sector workers. Franchised establishments will, by necessity, be involved.

It is important to assess from the franchisor whether any corporate or franchised stores in the system are the subject of a collective bargaining agreement, or are the subject of a certification drive by a union, or have already been certified. It may be that a certification drive in another part of the province could eventually affect the franchised business being acquired by you. This knowledge in advance will at least allow you to assess whether unionization of your franchised business would have any substantial or negative impact upon its economics or viability.

It is common knowledge that trade unions are moving into sectors such as retail and food services, and you should be aware of the potential for certification. Certainly in British Columbia (and perhaps other provinces), any actions or statements by you to dissuade a union certification may backfire by being deemed as an unfair labour practice. Caution, restraint, and legal advice are urged in these circumstances, together with aspirin.

8. GOOD FAITH, FAIRNESS, AND REASONABLENESS

The Ontario, PEI, and Alberta franchise laws impose a statutory duty of fair dealing in the performance and enforcement of the franchise agreement. The other provinces do not have such legislation but case law (that is, judge-made law) would indicate that there is a "common law" duty of good faith and fair dealing in some provinces, but the law is somewhat divided on this point.

It's important to note that it's not just the franchisor who must deal fairly with the franchisee. The franchisee must deal fairly with the franchisor as well. In my experience, there are ample cases of franchisees acting unfairly to the franchisor, underreporting or withholding royalties, deliberately not following the system, and carrying on the business in more or less permanent state of "cold war" with the franchisor. In other words, there are bad apples and bad actors among franchisees. Fairness and good faith, then, work in both ways. Franchisees who act unfairly and in bad faith will (and should) face the same legal sanctions as franchisors who do.

Regardless of whether you have an issue with the franchisor over some element of the franchise system you don't like, such as new requirements by the franchisor, interpretation of the operations manual, or for any other reason, withholding royalties, underreporting gross sales, undermining the franchised system, or misrepresenting information may well breach this duty of fair dealing as well as breach the franchise agreement. If it comes to litigation, such tactics won't look good in court and may well exacerbate your legal situation. Both you and the franchisor must act fairly under the agreement towards each other. You must take the high road.

While acting for franchisees "discussing" the franchise agreement before it is signed, I have, in some cases, been able to persuade franchisors to add a provision to their agreement to the effect that "the parties will deal with each other fairly and in good faith." "If it's the law anyway," I argue, with only a touch of embellishment, "why not state it in the agreement?"

If they aren't prepared to do this, my polite and measured response is: "Sorry, did I hear you correctly? You've made all sorts of representations and provided all sorts of comfort to my client about how fabulous this franchise is, how great the location is, how good the other franchisees in the system are, how successful the system is, and how you see the franchisees as your 'partners' and your 'family,' but you won't covenant in the agreement to treat the franchisee fairly and in good faith? Did I hear that correctly? Does that mean you want the right to treat them unfairly and in bad faith?"

I'm happy that most franchisors who I've "discussed" this with will agree to such a request. It needn't be done in the body of the agreement. It can be done in an addendum to the agreement (an addendum being a modification to the franchise agreement that forms a part of the agreement and is usually attached at the end of the document). It can also be in the form of a "letter agreement" as long as it's signed by both parties and acknowledged to be a modification of the agreement.

Although what might be called the standard Canadian form of franchise agreement usually provides for the franchisor acting reasonably in most circumstances in which it can exercise discretion (e.g., "the franchisor, acting reasonably shall … " or "subject to the reasonable approval of the franchisor") there may be issues in which you may want to add "reasonableness" language (e.g., "the franchisor, acting reasonably shall … " or "the parties, each acting reasonably and in good faith, shall … "). Remember, pick carefully and don't nitpick!

2

"BUYING" INTO THE FRANCHISE

By the time a prospective franchisee appears in his or her lawyer's office for advice concerning the acquisition of a franchise, one or more of the following things have likely occurred:

- The prospective franchisee has been to a trade show and has become interested in acquiring a particular franchise.

- The prospective franchisee has been surfing the Internet and has become interested in acquiring a particular franchise.

- The prospective franchisee has approached or been approached by a franchisor (or its sales agents) and has become interested in acquiring a franchise.

- The prospective franchisee has executed a deposit agreement and has paid between $2,000 and $10,000 towards the initial franchise fee (and has been given a copy of the formal franchise agreement to review).

- The prospective franchisee has signed the deposit agreement, paid a deposit, and executed the franchise agreement.

- The prospective franchisee has made or is about to make an offer to lease premises for the franchised business, including having paid or being about to pay a deposit to the landlord (or its leasing agents).

- The prospective franchisee has made or is about to make an arrangement to buy an existing franchise from another franchisee.

- The prospective franchisee has been given a copy of the franchisor's disclosure document.

- In very bad situations, the franchisee has already signed the franchise agreement.

If you are considering buying into a franchise, you should talk to a franchise lawyer before you sign any documents or pay any deposits or fees. My recommendation is that it should be a lawyer with experience with franchise law. This chapter will help you understand why it is important to consult a franchise lawyer as early as you can in the franchising process.

1. WHO ARE YOU DEALING WITH?

You can tell a little about a franchisor by knowing who the "sales force" is and how it "sells" its franchises. Is the seller a director, officer, or key employee of the franchisor? Is the seller employed directly by the franchisor or has the seller otherwise worked exclusively for this franchisor for a reasonable time period? Is the salesperson on "commission," meaning he or she gets paid when he or she "closes a deal"? Is the salesperson part of a brokerage network such that if you are not keen on acquiring a coffee franchise with headquarters in Seattle, the seller can sell you an extremely successful chicken concept hailing from Toronto, a low-carb wrap franchise catching on in Boston, or a pizza franchise with headquarters in Edmonton?

It may be that once the sales process has been concluded, and you have "bought in," the friendly and charming people who "sold" the franchise to you have somehow stopped returning phone calls and emails, and have moved on to the next customer or the next up and coming concept. To your surprise and trepidation, you must now deal with perhaps a less-than-friendly president of a less-than-friendly franchisor who has just quit smoking, suffers from gout, employs field personnel comprised of former wrestlers, and watches *The Apprentice* to relax. Needless to say, you may discover a change in the corporate culture from the charming and helpful sales force. In other words, you may have to deal with reality, and the reality may be different than you expected. It is important then, for you to know whom you will inevitably be dealing with in the franchising relationship and, to the extent possible, to be comfortable with those persons. If you aren't comfortable, why would you proceed?

Some franchisors have instigated what is euphemistically referred to as a "debunking" session (or a "discovery day"), whereby, prior to the execution of the franchise agreement (but after a deposit agreement has been signed, a deposit provided, and the prospective franchisee is ready to "sign on"), the president or senior managers of the franchisor send the sales force "out of the room" and tell the prospective franchisee words to the effect that, "I don't know and I don't care what he told you. He's just a commissioned sales guy. This is the way it is in this franchise. There are no guarantees you are going to make any money and it's hard work. And by the way, sign here, acknowledging that you understand this."

These sort of debunking sessions serve as a "reality check" for overeager franchisees who have been won over by the sales process and the salesperson, or have otherwise sold the deal to themselves. But these sessions also assist the franchisor by allowing a franchisor to claim that there were no representations or warranties made to the franchisee that weren't contained in the franchise agreement (i.e., "I told him the way it was").

2. DEPOSIT AGREEMENTS

Deposit agreements containing confidentiality covenants are, on the whole, an encouraging sign within the franchise relationship. Franchisors have legitimate interests to protect. The franchisor wishes to separate the serious contenders from the "tire kickers," and the litmus test for that purpose is the execution of a deposit agreement and the placing of a deposit. The tire kickers will move on to other franchises; the serious contenders will take the process further.

From the perspective of the franchisor, it not only wishes to separate the genuinely interested from the marginally interested, it also wishes to protect its system, concept, and intellectual property rights. The franchisor does not wish to enter into negotiations with you, provide you with a franchise agreement, a disclosure document, perhaps financial statements, and other confidential information, thus educating you on the secrets that led to the franchisor's success in the marketplace, only to have you back out of the deal and form a competing business across the street.

In Ontario, there can be no deposit agreements entered and no deposit made until the franchisor has made disclosure according to the *Arthur Wishart Act*, and waited the requisite 14-day period after disclosure.

In Alberta, a deposit can be taken before disclosure and a deposit agreement entered (usually with confidentiality provisions included), but the deposit must be no more than 20 percent of the franchisor's initial franchise fee and it must be fully refundable if the franchisee chooses not to proceed.

2.1 Who holds the deposit?

The most important practical problem at this stage is, who holds the deposit and how do you get it back if the deal falls apart? The deposit is going to be held by either the franchisor or the franchisor's commissioned salespersons. If you decide not to go further in the process, cannot acquire bank financing, or do not approve the location the franchisor has subsequently chosen and you request the deposit monies to be returned, the money may be difficult to get back. In some systems, the franchisor or its sales agents have already spent the deposit monies and are waiting for other deposit monies or initial franchise fees from other franchisees that will be used to repay you if you are seeking your money back. This could take months, and legal action respecting return of deposit monies is not cost-effective for you if you are forced to hire a lawyer to commence legal proceedings. So when you ask for the money back, it's gone, and it may be gone for some time. (By the way, this does not usually happen with Canada's established franchisors.)

One option is that if you are able to approach your lawyer in advance of signing the deposit agreement, deposit monies could be placed either in trust with your lawyer or in trust with the franchisor's lawyer on undertakings to return these monies immediately upon you deciding not to enter into the franchise agreement. Be aware that franchisors or their sales agents may delay the return of deposits for the aforementioned reason or to give one more try at the sales process.

For lawyers, nothing speaks louder than an undertaking, which is a contract between the lawyer accepting the undertaking and the person putting the lawyer on the undertaking. Lawyers who fail to comply with undertakings risk disciplinary action by their Law Society. Although some franchisors aren't fond of this approach, it is an efficient means of ensuring that the franchisor knows that you are serious while at the same time ensuring that if the deal does not proceed, the money hasn't been spent and can be returned quickly to you. It shows that if you're still just a tire kicker, you're a smart one!

Undertakings placed on lawyers have a way of focusing a lawyer's attention. Lawyers aren't keen on receiving disciplinary letters from their Law Societies, let alone disbarment. So its probably fair to consider holding the deposit in trust with a lawyer — even the franchisor's lawyer — when dealing with a start-up franchisor with a limited or non-existent track record, or if you are dealing with a start-up regional franchisee (i.e., a master franchisee for a province that is not the same entity that controls the US franchise rights), or if you're dealing with commissioned sales agents in the previously cited circumstances.

The well-known and established franchise companies don't normally spend the deposit monies before they receive the initial franchise fee. They aren't adding much to the bottom line by trying to keep $1,000 of your deposit money. I'd probably take the established franchisor's word that your money will be returned forthwith and I probably wouldn't put the deposit money in trust with a lawyer. (Most of Canada's established franchise community are members of the Canadian Franchise Association. If the franchisor you're dealing with isn't, ask why.)

The established and reputable franchisors will return the monies forthwith; however, certain deposit agreements may contain a provision whereby the franchisor is entitled to deduct a portion to compensate it for its administrative time. This portion may vary. Usually the agreement will say a reasonable amount and the parties are left figuring out what reasonable is. For example, if a franchisor kept $1,000 out of a $5,000 deposit, it wouldn't be unreasonable unless the deposit agreement said "fully refundable." This depends on the costs the franchisor has incurred.

As an aside, if there are significant conditions in the future to be satisfied by the franchisor (e.g., securing a location), having all or a portion of the initial franchise fee held in trust by your lawyer or the franchisor's lawyer may also be a means of "getting it back quickly" in the event the condition is not satisfied but the money has been paid.

2.2 Ontario and Alberta regulations on deposits

As noted above, Ontario and Alberta have specific regulations on deposits for the acquisition of franchises. In particular, no deposit can be taken by a franchisor for an Ontario franchise, and no agreement can be signed unless disclosure has been made pursuant to the Ontario *Arthur Wishart* legislation and the requisite time period has passed. A deposit agreement will be deemed to be a franchise agreement under that statute. (For more information about disclosure agreements, see Part 3.)

In Alberta, fully refundable deposits may be taken prior to disclosure by the franchisor, but only in an amount not more than 20 percent of the franchisor's initial franchise fee, and only where any deposit agreement is limited to dealing with the deposit, the location or territory, and confidentiality and non-use of the franchisor's information and materials.

Sample 1 is an example of a deposit agreement. It contains a few interesting errors.

Note that Sample 1 says the franchisee is in the province of Ontario. If this deposit agreement were actually entered with a franchisee for a location in the province of Ontario before the delivery of a disclosure document and the expiry of the 14-day cooling off period mandated under the *Arthur Wishart Act* (Franchise Disclosure), 2000, the statute would be breached and the franchisor may well have opened itself up to liability. Franchisors who grant franchises to franchisees in Ontario must not have the franchisee sign any agreement relating to the franchise, or take any money from the prospective franchisee prior to disclosure having been made in accordance with the Act and the expiry of the 14-day cooling off period.

As noted earlier, in Alberta, a deposit agreement is permitted, but the deposit must be non-refundable, must only contain provisions respecting confidentiality, and must be for no more than 20 percent of the franchisor's initial franchise fee. In the other common-law provinces, there are no similar requirements concerning deposits, so "buyer beware."

Note that the franchisor in this sample is entitled to retain some of the deposit monies to compensate it for administrative expenses (see paragraph 4 of Sample 1). If this happens in your deposit agreement, you need to ask yourself the following questions:

- How much is the deposit?

- When will the deposit be returned if the transaction fails to complete? (In Sample 1, the deposit agreement does not say.)

- Will it take a year before the deposit is returned?

Sometimes franchisors will legitimately want the right to deduct a portion of the deposit to pay for some of its expenses (e.g., location-related and design costs that have been incurred). That's a business decision you must make. If you are going to agree to that, then fix a dollar amount that you can live with and you are prepared to agree is non-refundable. You should fix a time period in which the money will be returned (i.e., five days from written notice).

What if the franchisor rejects the franchisee? Can it still retain part of the deposit monies to compensate it for its administrative expenses? (See paragraph 5 of Sample 1.) This is something else you should consider.

Note as well this franchisor is seeking to prevent the franchisee from competing with it if the franchise agreement is not entered (see clause in 2.[f.] in Sample 1). Restrictive covenants are interpreted very strictly by Canadian courts, which see them as restraints of trade and will not enforce them unless they are "reasonable" in the circumstances. Regardless whether the franchisor has breached Ontario law by having the franchisee enter into the deposit agreement prior to delivery of the disclosure document or waiting the requisite 14-day cooling off period, and regardless of the fact that this may breach Alberta law by requiring a deposit that is more than 20 percent of the franchisor's initial franchise fee, as this covenant lacks a time period and geographic boundaries for its restriction (i.e., one mile for one year), it will in all likelihood be unenforceable by the franchisor.

Note also in Sample 1 that the number of days don't match, which is a good indication that other things will be wrong as well.

SAMPLE 1
DEPOSIT AGREEMENT (ONTARIO)

EMMA & JEREMY'S INTERNET CAFÉ & DONUT EMPORIUM LTD.

DEPOSIT AGREEMENT (ONTARIO ONLY)

1. The Applicant, _____, hereby makes application to be considered for an Emma & Jeremy's franchise with the Franchisor, Emma & Jeremy's Internet Café & Donut Emporium Ltd. upon substantially the same terms and conditions as are set forth below and such other terms and conditions as are generally contained in the Franchisor's standard form of Franchise Agreement.

2. The Applicant understands that prior to executing the Franchise Agreement, the Franchisor may furnish information and material that will be of a confidential nature concerning the Franchisor and the franchise system including, without limitation, the contents of the Franchise Agreement, the Franchisor's operations and other manuals, and the Franchisor's training and other materials (the "Confidential Information"). The Applicant acknowledges that the Confidential Information is the property of the Franchisor and that —

    (a) it will not make or allow to be made copies of all or any part of the Confidential Information;

    (b) it will not publish or allow to be published all or any part of the Confidential Information;

    (c) it will not disclose or allow to be disclosed to any person, firm, or corporation, directly or indirectly, the contents of all or any part of the Confidential Information;

    (d) it will not retain all or any part of the Confidential Information and will return all of the Confidential Information to the Franchisor on demand;

    (e) it will not make any use of all or any part of the Confidential Information for its own purposes or for any purpose other than pursuant to an agreement reached with the Franchisor, and will keep and respect the confidentiality of the Confidential Information for so long as all or any part thereof shall remain confidential to the Franchisor;

    (f) it will not carry on any business similar to the franchised business in the event that the parties do not enter into a franchise agreement

3.   The Applicant encloses herewith a deposit in the amount of $ <u>10,000</u>. It is understood that if the Franchise Agreement is entered into between the Franchisor and the Applicant, such amount will be credited towards payment of the initial franchise fee without interest or deduction.

4.   Upon receipt of notice of acceptance of this Application from the Franchisor, the Applicant shall have <u>ten</u> (<u>5</u>) days in which to enter into the Franchise Agreement with the Franchisor, and pay the balance of the initial franchise fee of $ <u>30,000</u> . In the event that the Applicant fails to enter into the Franchise Agreement and pay the balance of the initial franchise fee within the above-mentioned time period, the Applicant understands and agrees that the deposit referred to in paragraph 3 hereof will be returned within a reasonable period of time to the Applicant with a reasonable set off for the Franchisor's administrative expenses.

5.   If the Franchisor fails to accept this Application within <u>ten</u> (<u>10</u>) days of the date hereof, the Applicant understands that the deposit referred to in paragraph 3 hereof will be returned within a reasonable period of time to the Applicant with a reasonable set off for the Franchisor's administrative expenses.

6.   The Applicant understands that the acceptance by the Franchisor of a deposit from the Applicant is no guarantee that the Applicant will be granted an Emma & Jeremy's franchise, and that the Franchisor may reject this application for any reason whatsoever.

DATED at the City of <u>Toronto</u>, in the Province of <u>Ontario</u>, this <u>5</u> day of <u>October</u>, 20—.

_____   _____
Applicant *(Signature)*   Witness *(Signature)*

_____   _____
(Print Name)   *(Print Name)*
~~~~~~

Emma & Jeremy's Internet Café & Donut Emporium Ltd. hereby acknowledges the foregoing together with the receipt of the amount of the deposit referred to above and agrees to consider the Applicant as a candidate for an Emma & Jeremy's franchise.

DATED at the City of <u>Toronto</u>, in the Province of <u>Ontario</u>, this <u>5</u> day of October, 20—.

Emma & Jeremy's Internet Café & Donut Emporium Ltd.

Per:_____

3. ARE THE INITIAL FEE AND OTHER COSTS IN US OR CANADIAN DOLLARS?

For US franchisors (who may not have converted their US agreement and marketing material to a Canadian format), initial fees and other costs set out in the franchisor's US FDD or in US-based pro forma financial statements will be in US, not Canadian dollars, and will be based on the franchisor's US experience, not a Canadian one. Needless to say, those costs will be different in the US and won't factor in the GST, PST, HST, Canadian tax rates, lease costs, labour costs, or other differing costs.

A pro forma financial statement is a projection of what the franchisor thinks or expects the location to reflect in the first year (or the time period in the projection). It is little more than a projection, and like the weather, can be quite accurate or highly inaccurate. Actual financials are more reliable as they reflect actual performance over a period of time, rather than estimating performance. Accordingly, buying an existing operation from a franchisee or an outlet run by the franchisor itself as a corporate location (with actual financials to read) has its benefits. Also, you should inquire how the franchisor calculated its pro forma statements, especially if it has no operating locations of its own.

If the franchisor has simply extrapolated US assumptions regarding anticipated Canadian sales (and costs of sales), this may also be unrealistic in Canada. The franchisor's numbers may simply reflect the US experience. Taking the US population and dividing it by ten to deal with a Canadian population that is one-tenth the size of its southern neighbour is not always an accurate way to measure anticipated performance in Canada. Canada is a country in which our disposable income is less, our labour costs are higher, and our taxes are more than what they would be in the US. As a nation, we don't seem to shop or eat out as often as Americans do, so pro forma financial statements that assume that a sample group of 200,000 Canadians will shop and eat out as often as a sample of 200,000 Americans may well be flawed. Mind you, this doesn't mean you have to treat financial or pro forma financial statements based solely on US performance as if they were claims for weapons of mass destruction, but you should treat them with a healthy degree of skepticism and an ever so small grain of salt. Your accountant may be able to assist you with this. So might other franchisees, particularly in Canada.

4. ROYALTIES

Franchise agreements will almost always contain some form of royalty, which is a monetary amount payable to the franchisor by you every week or every month, depending on the agreement. The continuing royalty keeps the franchisor financially able to administer the franchise system. Franchisors need royalties as much as franchisees need profit from sales.

Although one often sees royalty rates of between 5 and 8 percent in the restaurant industry, this may not be appropriate in other industries. It may be wise to make inquiries of franchisees within different franchise systems in the same industry if the royalty rate is considered too high in the circumstances. Often, start-up franchisors have no scientific method to their selection of the initial franchise fee and royalty amounts; they simply pick what they think the going rate is. If the "going rate" for that industry is less in other systems, perhaps this is worthy of discussion with the franchisor. Consulting a publication such as the current year's edition of *The Franchise Annual* will give you an overview of what the going rates are in various business categories.

Note that franchisors will often have a clause in the agreement that provides that under no circumstances will the franchisee "withhold any royalty or other payment due and owing to the franchisor." It goes without saying then, that in the absence of special circumstances, failure to pay royalties is normally considered a material breach of the franchise agreement that could lead to the franchisee's termination by the franchisor. (See Chapter 8 for more information about royalties.)

5. WITHHOLDING TAXES ON ROYALTIES

It is important that the US franchisor (or any other non-Canadian franchisor) understands that the Canadian franchisee has an obligation to deduct withholding taxes on the royalties and similar monies owed to the non-Canadian franchisor and remit them to Canada Revenue Agency (CRA). Withholding tax requirements are in place to make sure that the taxes are paid before the funds are paid to the non-Canadian franchisor. As a franchisee, you are required to withhold approximately 15 percent of the royalties or other payments to the franchisor and send them to the CRA.

Should you, as the franchisee, have to pay more than the stipulated amount of royalties just because the franchisor did not contemplate that withholding taxes would have to be paid? After all, the non-Canadian franchisor could have created a Canadian subsidiary and effectively avoided this problem.

The US-based franchisor will always take the position that you, the franchisee, are responsible for paying the withholding tax. The addition of this extra tax might not make the venture ecomonic for you. CRA will assess you, the franchisee, in the event the withholding tax is not paid. This is an important issue to address with all non-Canadian franchisors and should be resolved before you sign the agreement.

6. LIMITED LIABILITY COMPANY

Often, the franchisee will be a limited liability company, which is also called a corporation. A limited liability company is a distinct legal entity that exists at law separately from its shareholders, officers, and directors. This means that the shareholders, officers, and directors of a company are not personally responsible for the debts and obligations of their company unless they specifically agree to be responsible for such debts and obligations (e.g., by way of a personal covenant or personal guarantee).

In very limited circumstances, certain statutes (particularly environmental and tax statutes) can impose personal liability on directors, shareholders, and officers of a company, making such persons liable for the company's debts, although this "piercing of the corporate veil" is not common.

The issue here is that you would probably prefer not to sell the house and liquidate the RRSPs if the venture fails. By incorporating a limited liability company and operating the franchised business through that company, personal liability for the company's debts can be minimized, unless you agreed to assume those liabilities personally by way of a guarantee or personal covenant.

There are also tax-planning reasons why a franchised business such as this one might be operated through a company (i.e., dividends are treated differently for tax purposes than employment income from wages, and there are potential tax planning strategies that are better suited to a corporate entity).

Another reason why a company is often used as the franchisee has to do with banks; banks and other commercial lenders sometimes require their business loans to be made to corporations, even though the borrower may be borrowing the money in his or her personal capacity for an inexpensive franchise. The bank's lending policies may require that the loan originate from its commercial loans department, rather than from the personal loans department (the latter handling your mortgage or car loan).

The commercial loans department makes all of its loans to corporations; so they normally require you to be incorporated because that's what the department is streamlined to do. The bank's own internal policies may dictate that you have to use a company so that it can loan to your company.

Sometimes, the franchisor will require the franchisee to be a living, breathing person (or persons), not a company. However, the "individual" franchisee will be permitted to assign and transfer the franchise agreement to a company that he or she personally owns. This is one way the franchisor can obtain a personal covenant, like a guarantee, where a living, breathing person (and not an inanimate entity like a corporation) signs on the dotted line and puts themselves personally "on the hook" for any money owing to the franchisor.

7. YOUR PERSONAL LIABILITY

Some franchise agreements will be drafted such that a corporation that you have created is in fact the "franchisee" under the franchise agreement and that the obligations of your corporation under the agreement are guaranteed by you in your personal capacity. In other words, you, as guarantor, will be called on to pay the obligations of your company under the franchise agreement if your company doesn't pay.

Other agreements are structured in reverse. That is, you are the individual with whom the franchisor is principally dealing and you are entitled, after execution of the franchise agreement, to assign your interest to a company that you own. In this way, you (being the individual who signed the contract in your personal capacity) will still be personally liable for the obligations of the corporate franchisee if your company fails to pay its obligations to the franchisor, but you are allowed to run the franchise through your company for tax and related reasons. Indeed, through a company you may reduce your exposure and liability to third parties. But as you originally entered the franchise agreement personally, you are still personally responsible even though you "assigned" it to your company.

Still another form of structure gaining some popularity is one in which both you and your company are collectively referred to as the "franchisee." Remember, your company is a separate legal personality, just like you are. Here, you and your company are on the hook: your company is the franchisee but you are also the franchisee (e.g., Mr. Smith *and* Smithco Ltd. both signed on as franchisees and are each liable to perform their covenants and obligations under the agreement). It's done because there are defences available to guarantors at law that might not be available to franchisees who entered the agreement in their personal capacitates. The franchisor could bring an action against you as "franchisee" or your company as "franchisee," and it would probably bring an action against both of you, on the basis that if your company has no money, you might.

Other agreements have far more ephemeral language. They don't refer to the guarantor of the agreement being a guarantor. Instead, they refer to the person signing the agreement in his or her personal capacity as "associate." Whether they are called "associate" or otherwise, generally, if someone signs a franchise agreement in his or her personal capacity (i.e., using his or her personal name), he or she will be personally bound (giving credence to the old legal adage "you sign it, you eat it").

Obviously, as a prospective franchisee, you should consider speaking to an accountant or tax lawyer about possible tax consequences in respect of each form of organization.

7.1 Spouses as "franchisee"

All too often spouses who jointly own the franchisee corporation and jointly guarantee the obligations of the corporation, or the husband and wife jointly sign as "franchisee" in their personal capacities.

Given that not all such business opportunities succeed, would you, as a prospective franchisee, really wish to have your spouse exposed to this potential liability? This is especially so where only one of you will be actively involved in the franchised business. In other words, if a guarantee or personal covenant is required, must both you and your spouse take on the potential exposure? Or should only one of you be the covenanting party, taking the risk and being prepared to take the loss; the other party being shielded from such loss?

Too often, one spouse, even with independent legal advice, signs a franchise agreement as guarantor, co-franchisee, or associate, but has minimal or non-existent involvement in or knowledge about the management of the business. A failed business means both parties are subject to possible execution against their personal assets, which may include the family home and perhaps retirement savings. So perhaps only one spouse should give the guarantee or personal covenant. In these circumstances, it's worth clarifying with the franchisor.

Finally, in respect of a personal guarantee or covenant, is it possible to "cap" the exposure at a limited amount of money or a limited number of months worth of royalties? This is also worth discussing with the franchisor.

8. DOES THE FRANCHISOR OWN THE TRADE-MARKS?

Does the franchisor own the trade-marks? You can check this relatively easily by performing your own "bare bones" trade-mark search at the Canadian Trade-Marks Database, which is maintained by Strategis: http://strategis.ic.gc.ca/cipo/trademarks/search/tmSearch.do. Or simply put CIPO into a search engine and it will direct you to the Canadian Intellectual Property Office, where you can find the trade-marks page. This website contains a lot of useful information on matters dealing with the federal government, but the most important matter here is that the site maintains a database for all registered, expunged, current, and pending Canadian trade-marks.

Enter the name of franchisor's trade-mark in the search engine and assess from the results whether the mark has matured to registration or whether it has been applied for only (meaning the examiner at the trade-marks office is still assessing the trade-mark application and its potential for registration). You can also check if the mark has neither been applied for nor registered.

Note that Strategis Canadian Trade-Mark Database searches are not always foolproof or perfect. Garbage in will yield garbage out, so make sure you enter the trade-mark accurately. Also, the search engine has limitations, chiefly the fact that it finds "dead hits" but rarely does it find phonetic or visual equivalents (e.g., easy vs. EZ or Pharma vs. Farm).

If the mark has not matured to registration, meaning it does not have a registration number with initials (the initials are almost always TMA) immediately preceding the number, it is possible that the mark might not be approved or might be opposed by an interested third party (usually the owner of a similar mark). This might cause the franchisor to have to pick another mark and "re-brand" the franchise at some late (and more inconvenient) time. Re-branding can create confusion in the system and necessitate a change of signage, advertising, and other branding identifiers.

It is important to consider what will happen if the franchisor does not have a registered trade-mark at the time you acquire the franchise rights and if the franchisor might not ever be able to secure the trade-mark. It might be prevented from ever obtaining the trade-mark that you think you're getting the right to use. The question to ask yourself is, "Is it worth all that money for this franchise if the franchisor can't legally license me its trade-mark and brand?"

If you are still considering signing the agreement, then ask yourself this: "Who pays for re-branding if the mark, and all that goes along with it, has to change?"

In such cases, I like to have an agreement from the franchisor that if its trade-mark isn't registered at the time the agreement is entered, then the franchisor is responsible for the costs of new signage and other display items arising from the need for this new mark. This could be done by way of an indemnity from the franchisor.

3
MASTER FRANCHISING

1. WHAT IS MASTER FRANCHISING?

In any negotiation with a "franchisor," it is important to determine the relationship between all the players. Who are you contracting with? If it's not a well-known franchisor with a recognizable world-wide brand, then who are you dealing with, and what rights does this person have?

Some franchisees will not acquire their franchise rights from the franchisor (or who they expect the "franchisor" to be). In some cases, their franchise contract will be with the franchisor's Canadian branch or subsidiary, or one of its affiliated Canadian corporations. This is because many franchisors will not franchise directly out of the worldwide head office in the United States or the UK, but instead will create a Canadian subsidiary or affiliate that will run the franchisor's franchised and corporate operations in Canada. This structure is adopted in other countries as well.

In Canada, this is done for a variety of reasons (including tax planning) and helps deal with Canadians withholding taxes. Where the US-based franchisor has created a Canadian subsidiary, that subsidiary may have a Canadian office and hire Canadian management personnel, although this is not, strictly speaking, necessary. Certainly in larger and more established franchise systems, it is normal to have a "Canadian" office that Canadian franchisees can deal with, as opposed to dealing with someone in Fort Lauderdale, Edinburgh, or Melbourne, who might lack knowledge of the Canadian marketplace, not appreciate the size of the Canadian market (let alone the weather), and be many time zones and long plane flights away.

In other instances, franchisees will be contracting with a "master franchisee" for its franchise rights. (Sometimes the term "master franchisor" is used to denote the area franchisor granting franchise rights in a territory. More often the term "master franchisee" is used.) A "master franchisee" is similar to a franchisee, only the master franchisee will have additional rights and responsibilities and a much larger territory. Instead of the franchisor granting the master franchisee the right to establish one franchised outlet in one mall in a city with 12 other franchised outlets from the same system, the franchisor is normally granting the locally based master franchisee the right to —

- establish numerous outlets on its own account throughout a large territory (say for example, all of Ontario or all of Canada); and

- sub-franchise the franchisor's system and enter into individual franchise agreements with other entities (called sub-franchises or unit franchises).

The concept works well. Many US- or Canadian-based franchisors may lack the financial resources to expand to other territories and into other countries. Contracting with a locally based territorial master franchisee allows the "head franchisor" to expand the brand in the new territory using the "local knowledge" of the master franchisee, as well as the master franchisee's risk capital and the master franchisee's infrastructure (i.e., employees, offices, etc.). Risk is spread to the master franchisee. The locally based master franchisee will usually have some experience of the local market that the franchisor might not possess (i.e., they're Canadian), and the master franchisee will often be situated in the territory, as opposed to being in Fort Lauderdale, Melbourne, or Los Angeles.

In Canada, some franchisors will divide up the country on a provincial or regional basis and grant master franchise rights to a master franchisee in respect of "Western Canada" or the "Maritimes" and that master franchisee will be charged with franchising the "XYZ concept" in those provinces while the franchisor retains the right to develop its own stores and to franchise in Ontario, Quebec, and indeed, the rest of the world.

There may be overriding reasons why a franchisor (even a Canadian one) may wish to master franchise the province of Quebec; certainly language, culture, and other distinct nuances of Quebec's society might lead a franchisor to contract with a Quebec company, with principals and employees fluent in French, to enter unit franchise agreements in that province (in French) and service the franchise network (again, in French).

Not only does it make sense for franchisor to master franchise a territory where it may well need specialized local knowledge with respect to the territory (again, the example of Quebec comes to mind with its civil law system and language), but master franchising is also an appropriate means of expanding the brand when the franchisor does not have the financial or human resources to adequately do so. For example, a Vancouver-based franchisor may want to expand into the Ontario marketplace but understands that Toronto is a five-hour plane flight, 3,366 kilometres, and three time zones from the West Coast. Besides, Vancouver is just too nice to have to leave it in February and March when all the flowers are blooming and there's still snow on the ground everywhere else in the country!

From the franchisor's perspective, it may be difficult to solicit new franchisees let alone service existing ones very well if there is no presence in the "faraway territory." Although travelling between BC and Ontario may be good for someone's frequent flyer points, distance makes it difficult to promptly service an existing territory or expand into a new one. (You just can't drive there in an hour for a meeting or a surprise visit, so out of sight can truly be out of mind.) Master franchising allows the franchisor to rely upon the skills, acumen, risk capital, infrastructure, and local knowledge of someone within the territory to solicit for new franchisees, open stores on its own account, and service existing franchisees.

Unit franchisees should be aware that their contract will normally be with the master franchisee and not with the so called "head franchisor." Accordingly, the master franchisee is the only party the unit franchisee can obtain a legal remedy from because the franchisor in the US or the UK isn't a party to that agreement. The franchisor in Fort Lauderdale does not want a phone call from a disgruntled unit franchisee in Winnipeg. It's the master franchisee's franchisee; it's the master franchisee's problem. Unit franchise agreements that contemplate the existence of a master franchisee will normally contain a provision that provides that if the master franchisee should ever be terminated, the franchisor will step into the shoes of the master franchisee. All royalties and other monies due and owing to the master franchisee will then be payable to the franchisor and not the master franchisee.

2. COST OF BECOMING A MASTER FRANCHISEE

It is beyond the scope of this book to advise on master franchise agreements or to analyze a master franchise agreement in the same detail that we are analyzing the unit franchise agreement in Part 2. Suffice to say, however, that the cost to acquire master franchise rights for a province or a group of provinces (or for that matter a part of a province or the boundaries of a large city) will be larger than what would be charged to acquire the franchise rights for one location only. The franchisor may do an analysis of the territory and determine that the master franchised territory will be able to support 40 outlets over a ten-year period.

Perhaps the price to acquire master franchise rights will be a product of the franchisor's forgone income in not exploiting the territory itself. The price might be some factor of 40 initial franchise fees and 40 royalty streams.

From practical experience, when a master franchisee is franchising individual locations to the "unit franchisees" or "sub-franchisees," the initial franchise fee and royalties may well be higher than if the franchisor was doing this on its own account. For example, a US-based franchisor may charge $25,000 USD for the rights to open a XYZ bagel emporium in the city of Seattle. If the US franchisor has entered into a master franchise agreement with a British Columbia-based company to master franchise the same concept in BC, the initial franchise fee may in fact be the equivalent of $30,000 USD; the $5,000 differential being paid to the franchisor on the signing of each unit franchise agreement.

The royalties may also be slightly higher for Canadian unit franchisees when compared to their US counterparts who franchise directly from the "head franchisor." This is because the Canadian master franchisee will normally have to pay a percentage of the royalty it collects from individual franchisees to the franchisor.

3. PERFORMANCE AND DEVELOPMENT OBLIGATIONS OF THE MASTER FRANCHISEE

The master franchisee will normally have "development obligations" under its agreement with the head franchisor. Such development obligations will often prescribe that "so many" stores will be opened in the first year followed by a higher number in the second and a still higher number in the third year. Failure to meet these performance obligations might well lead to the termination of the master franchise agreement (and the master franchisee's rights) or the franchisor could reduce the size of the master's territory or make the territory "non-exclusive," entering into other master franchise agreements with other entities.

In order to meet such performance obligations (or because it wishes to reserve the best locations for itself), the master franchisee in the territory may decide to open up its own "corporate" locations that will also be subject to a sub-franchise or unit franchise agreement in each case. It is desirable that the master franchisee have some corporate stores, if for any other reason, to have day-to-day familiarity with the business just like the franchisees.

4. NEGOTIATING A UNIT FRANCHISE AGREEMENT WITH A MASTER FRANCHISEE

It may be difficult, if not impossible, to negotiate the unit franchise agreement with a master franchisee, not because master franchisees are inherently difficult and unaccommodating people, but because their contract with the franchisor may prohibit or severely restrict the master franchisee's rights to modify the unit franchise agreement. Normally, the form of unit franchise agreement the franchisor requires its master franchisee to use (with the master's unit franchisees) is appended to the master's contract with a requirement not to modify the form without the franchisor's prior written consent. US-based franchisors are very reluctant to agree to change any part of their agreements for the following four main reasons:

1. They don't want wacky, one-off side deals floating around the known world.

2. "This is my contract, and if you don't like it, find another franchise."

3. They don't want franchisees comparing who got the better deal and coming back to the franchisor to negotiate different deals.

4. Separate deals may adversely effect their own disclosure obligations under US franchise laws.

There are variations on this agreement, such as in cases in which an individual or corporation is not granted master franchise rights, per se, but rather is granted the right to find prospects, sign up franchisees who sign an agreement with the franchisor, and service existing franchisees within the territory in exchange for a portion of the initial franchise fee and a portion of the ongoing royalties, or on some other financial arrangement. This might be called a multi-unit area franchise.

PART 2

THE FRANCHISE AGREEMENT

4

EVERYTHING YOU EVER WANTED TO KNOW ABOUT A FRANCHISE AGREEMENT BUT WERE AFRAID TO ASK

Otto von Bismarck's oft quoted remark, "Laws are like sausages: it is better not to see them made," might also be applied to the drafting of franchise agreements.

Franchise agreements are written by lawyers at great expense to their franchisor clients. Accordingly, one would expect that most franchise agreements would be drafted in favour of franchisors. Generally, this is the case, and it shows in circumstances in which the franchise agreement is so demanding and overbearing that virtually every element of the business relationship is governed by the agreement. A 75-page franchise agreement may be the crowning achievement of the franchisor's counsel who has drafted for every possible contingency except one: The franchisor can't sell the agreement in the marketplace because potential franchisees are too intimidated by the length and onerousness of the contract. Accordingly, there are franchisors who appreciate that franchisees shouldn't (and won't) sign an agreement simply because it's placed in front of them. The market may persuade franchisors to make their agreements shorter, simpler, and less onerous.

Still other franchisors have adopted what might be called a "user friendly" or "folksy" drafting style using simple language and incorporating reasonableness wherever the franchisor's discretion or approval is called for. For example, the following language from a recent franchise agreement I worked on sets the tone for the entire agreement:

Our Agreement has been written in an informal style to help you understand and become familiar with all of its provisions before you sign it. Accordingly, in this Agreement we refer to _____ [Franchisor] as "we," "us," or "ourselves" or in some cases as the "Franchisor." We refer to you as "you" or in some cases as the "Franchisee" ...

Regardless of the type of franchise agreement that has been presented to you, franchisors pay many thousands of dollars to their lawyers to prepare and regularly revise the franchisor's standard form of franchise agreement, and it should be expected that the franchise agreement is always written for the benefit of the franchisor.

Most Canadian agreements in circulation these days have what I might call a standard "Canadian" flavor to them. This may in part be explained by the fact that there are at present no more than 50 Canadian lawyers who can be said to specialize in this area of law or who have otherwise made it the primary focus of their practice (circa 2009). Perhaps, as lawyers, we've all seen everyone else's franchise agreement somewhere and we've all adopted a similar format. (I can usually recognize the original author of a franchise agreement within the first few minutes of my review.)

Chapters 4 through 14 explain the standard types of clauses that you may come across in a typical Canadian franchise agreement. The sections of the agreement have been divided into chapters for easier readability, and the numbering of each section has been preserved to reflect the continuity of the agreement. You will find each section of the agreement in a grey box. Below the box, you will find commentary that should assist you in understanding the clause, and if appropriate, negotiating the clause as well. The commentary is deliberately general in nature and written for the general reader, so it's not meant to be as legally comprehensive as what you would find in a legal text book.

I have also deliberately incorporated certain provisions that are either inappropriate or just plain wrong to illustrate a point. Remember, many provisions of franchise agreements will not be negotiated by a franchisor, and approaching the franchisor with a list of 35 modifications is simply going to lead the franchisor to abandon you, your money, and your 35 points for someone else who is less of a bother. Picking your best five or six "deal points" and leaving the boilerplate "as is" is often a good strategy with franchisors, many of whom never "negotiate" (but often say they "clarify" their agreements). In other words, pick, don't nitpick!

If you are using a lawyer (which, despite this book, is still a wise and prudent idea), get a sense as to whether the lawyer you select is going to nit and pick at the boilerplate, or, at the very least, will explain the agreement so that you understand what you are getting into (and at the very most, get you the best deal that you can get). If you are engaging a lawyer, I strongly recommend you hire a lawyer familiar with franchise law.

EMMA & JEREMY'S
FRANCHISE AGREEMENT

EMMA & JEREMY'S
INTERNET CAFÉ & DONUT EMPORIUM LTD.

(Franchisor)

TO

_____

Full Corporate Name of Franchisee — if a corporation

(Corporate Franchisee)

AND

_____

Full Name of Guarantor or Guarantors

(Guarantor)

Franchise Agreement Number: _____

Expiry Date: _____

Date of this Agreement: _____

Province of Grant: _____

Date Disclosure Document delivered: _____

Who is the franchisor under this agreement? Did the franchisor "originate" the concept itself or did it acquire its rights to franchise the concept from another company and is therefore an "area franchisor"? Or does the franchisor have "master franchise" rights from another entity, perhaps out of the United States or the UK? If so, it can lose its rights to the franchised system if it is not in compliance under its own master franchise agreement with its "franchisor."

Who are you dealing with on the acquisition of the franchise? Are you dealing with a representative of the franchisor in your negotiations, or are you dealing with an independent salesperson (who likely earns a commission from the sale)? In other words, are the people you are dealing with when negotiating the agreement the same people you will be dealing with once the agreement is signed and the honeymoon is over? (See Chapter 2 for more information.)

Often, the franchisee will be a limited liability company, which is also called a corporation. (See Chapter 2 for more information on limited liability companies.)

AND:

NAME OF GUARANTOR(S), individuals with a residential address at

_____

(hereinafter collectively called the "Guarantor")

OF THE THIRD PART

Sometimes, instead of the word "Guarantor," you might also see the words "Associate" or "Individual Franchisee" in this spot. In either case, if the agreement is signed in one's personal capacity, there will be a personal agreement (sometimes called a personal covenant), which is an obligation by a person (or persons) to the effect that such person (or persons) will be liable to the franchisor (and perhaps others) in the event the corporation actually owned by the "Individual Franchisee" or "Associate" isn't able to perform his or her contractual obligations or pay his or her debts to the franchisor or others. In short, if an individual is a "party" to this agreement in his or her personal capacity, he or she will be "on the hook" in his or her personal capacity. This means he or she will have to pay the franchisor the money owed to it from his or her own personal resources if the franchisee corporation he or she has created cannot pay the franchisor the money owed to it.

Some form of guarantee or personal covenant is virtually always required by franchisors. The question is, can the guarantee be "capped" in terms of a dollar amount or capped in terms of years, or otherwise limited? Open-ended guarantees may be intimidating. Are you personally guaranteeing $5,000 or $500,000? Perhaps if the guarantee were capped at a sum that an individual could live with, one could sleep better at night. In other words, it may be better to know you have a personal monetary obligation of, for example, $50,000, than a personal obligation that could exceed that amount five-fold. Certainty as to your exposure could give you far more comfort than uncertainty, and may assist you in your own risk assessment of the venture.

Banks, it should be known, would never entertain a capping of the personal guarantee for their loans to you, but a franchisor just might agree to put a limit on its guarantee, especially a "start-up" franchisor with only a few franchisees, eager to establish more locations in a territory where it does not have a presence. However, some capping of personal liability from a bank loan may be available under the Small Business Improvement Loans Program (SBIL), underwritten by the Federal Government. Your personal liability under such program may be limited to 25 percent of the outstanding balance of the loan. See your banker for more details.

A. The Franchisor has developed a distinctive format, system and plan for the establishment, development and operation of an Internet café and donut shop under the trade-mark "EMMA & JEREMY'S" (such format, system and plan is hereinafter sometimes called the "System" or the "EMMA & JEREMY'S System");

Franchisors always claim that they have developed a unique format and system. It's up to you to determine whether the system is so unique that the concept will succeed in the marketplace or that it's so unique it's doomed to failure because the market is too small. In this example, we have a concept that is a donut shop and an Internet café. If you were considering signing this contract, you might ask yourself the following questions:

- Is this a business model with a future or does this franchise have a problem with its core business? Is it an Internet café selling donuts or a donut store with a few computers and a WiFi connection? Can Tim Hortons or Krispy Kreme end your business overnight with a WiFi connection and a few computers?

- Does an Internet café and donut shop have "legs" or is it a flash in the pan?

- Might current trends have a negative impact on the business model (e.g., the low-carb Atkins diet)?

- How many locations are there? How many are forecast? Have any failed or been terminated?

- Has the franchisor successfully operated one or more locations itself? In other words, has the franchisor been behind the till and stocked the shelves? Will the franchisor be in the trenches like you?

- Are there actual financial statements that might give you a clearer idea of how well one or more locations are performing? Or are the statements pro-forma statements that are just the franchisor's best guess as to the expected (and hoped for) performance at the location?

- What do the existing franchisees have to say about the franchisor and the concept? Are there franchisees with more than one outlet? (This is a good sign.)

- Are these franchisees making money or are they losing money? (The franchisees may not answer this question.)

- Would these franchisees buy into the concept again if they had to do it all over again?

• Are they happy? (Zen and pop psychology aside, this is a fundamentally important question to ask a franchisee.)

> B.   The Franchisor has registered with the Canadian Intellectual Property Office the trade-mark "EMMA & JEREMY'S," and "E & J's and DESIGN," and is the owner and user of other unregistered related trade-marks and trade names used in connection with the franchised business licensed hereunder (such trade-marks are hereinafter called the "Trade-marks");

Does the franchisor really own or otherwise control the trade-marks? You can check this by performing a trade-mark search at Strategis (http://strategis.ic.gc.ca/cipo/trademarks/search/tmSearch.do) or other trade-mark search engines. See Chapter 2 for more information on trade-mark ownership.

> C.   The Franchisee understands that the format, systems, food preparation techniques, specifications, standards, policies, and controls established and insisted upon by the Franchisor are fundamental to the EMMA & JEREMY'S System, and are for the purposes of establishing and maintaining certain standards of uniformity and quality control among all Franchisor owned and franchised EMMA & JEREMY'S Internet Café & Donut Emporiums, in order to maintain the proprietary rights to the EMMA & JEREMY'S System and Trade-marks for the benefit of the Franchisor and its Franchisees; and

> D.   The Franchisee and the Guarantors have applied for a franchise to operate an EMMA & JEREMY'S Internet Café & Donut Emporium utilizing the Franchisor's System at the franchised location set out herein, and based upon the representation of the Franchisee and the Guarantors, the Franchisor has agreed to grant such a franchise upon the terms and conditions of this Agreement.

This is a recital outlining what the parties have bargained for and referring to the representations made. Note that the franchisees *and* the guarantors have made application to acquire a franchise.

Note also that they have made representations to the franchisor in the sales process. Likely, the franchisee (or its principals) have provided net worth and other financial data to the franchisor to persuade the franchisor that they have the financial wherewithal to acquire and run the franchised business. If the franchisee has cooked up his or her financial and other credentials, it's likely a breach of the agreement which deserves, I'd argue, the same fate as a franchisor who has misrepresented facts to the franchisee!

NOW THEREFORE THIS AGREEMENT WITNESSES that in consideration of the promises and of the mutual covenants and agreements herein contained, and for other good and valuable consideration (the receipt and sufficiency of which is acknowledged by the parties), the parties agree as follows:

Although considered "boilerplate," this is an important clause, and you'll find it in virtually all franchise agreements. As a matter of contract law, courts only enforce contracts where there is consideration or "value" exchanged between the parties. This sentence reiterates that there is value exchanged and there is a commercial bargain enforceable by the courts.

5
GRANT AND TERM

1.   GRANT AND TERM

1.1   Grant of Franchise Rights

The Franchisor hereby grants to the Franchisee the non-exclusive license to operate a franchised EMMA & JEREMY'S Internet Café & Donut Emporium utilizing the Franchisor's business method, format, systems and Trade-marks at and from the franchised location specified in this Agreement upon the strict terms and conditions of this Agreement, and the Franchisee hereby accepts such grant (the franchised EMMA & JEREMY'S business conducted from the Franchised Location by the Franchisee is hereinafter referred to as the "Franchised Business").

This clause grants you, as the franchisee, the right to be an Emma & Jeremy's franchisee pursuant to the terms of the franchise agreement. What is the franchisor granting to you? Do you "buy" these rights the same way you'd buy (and own) a house or a car? Well, no, you don't. That's because the wording of the "grant" is expressed in terms of a "right, licence, and privilege to operate the franchised business for the term and to use the system and the trade-mark in connection therewith."

So that you're not misled, you are acquiring a licence to use a method or system and to operate the franchisor's business format and to use the franchisor's trade-marks. The agreement never says you buy the rights or that you have an ownership interest in the franchised system. Eventually, this grant expires. It is not by definition a permanent relationship. You have the use of the franchisor's business system and trade-marks for a time, and then those rights expire. To misquote a crude old joke and take it quite out of context: Franchises are like beer: you never "buy" it, you rent it!

1.2   Franchised Location

The specific franchised location to be licensed to the Franchisee is <u>2709 Victor Court, Victor Court Mall, Burlington, Ontario, Canada</u> (hereinafter called the "Franchised Location" or sometimes the "Franchised Location Premises").

Sometimes the actual premises won't be known for some time, as the franchisor is still attempting to secure a location, but you may still want to sign a franchise agreement "for the next available location." Beware of signing before you have secured a location, as "the next available location" may be unacceptable to you or the lease may be far more expensive than you first might have expected. In these circumstances, you could sign the franchise agreement in advance of the location being selected, but have the option to terminate the franchise agreement without penalty if a location is not secured, say, within 90 days, or you are not satisfied with the location the franchisor has chosen, or you determine that the terms of the lease are unacceptable.

Perhaps in such cases, the "initial franchise fee" could be held in trust by a lawyer, refundable to you in the event you decide not to proceed owing to an unacceptable location or a bad lease. (See Chapter 2, section **2.1** for more information on a lawyer holding the deposit or franchise fee in trust.)

1.3   Limitation on Territorial Protection

Subject to the Franchisor's rights under section 1.5 and 1.6 herein, and so long as the Franchisee is not in default under this Agreement, the Franchisor shall not own, operate, or franchise any other EMMA & JEREMY'S Internet Café & Donut Emporium that is located within a <u>five (5) kilometre radius of the Franchised Location Premises</u> (the "Protected Territory"). The Franchisee acknowledges the limited nature of the protection granted hereby, and that the Franchisor is not granting an exclusive trading territory to the Franchisee, but rather is granting to the Franchisee a territory around the Franchised Location that is protected from having another EMMA & JEREMY'S Internet Café & Donut Emporium located directly within it except in accordance with this agreement and specifically section 1.5 hereof. Further, the Franchisor and its other Franchisees are free to solicit customers for their respective franchised businesses from anywhere, including from within the Protected Territory.

Some franchisors (particularly, the larger, well-known franchisors) don't like to grant protected or exclusive territories, as it restricts the franchisor's ability to expand the franchised business to new locations and grant new agreements to new franchisees (e.g., a fabulous new mall becomes available after the location in question has been chosen and opened, but that new mall is on the other side of the street and therefore outside of the natural trading area of the existing franchisee). Many franchisors will, in my experience, entertain some form of territorial protection. Asking for territorial protection is not an unreasonable request, and one that franchisors expect. Whether they grant it or not is another matter.

Perhaps you will discover the franchisor's policy from discussion with existing franchisees, if they are willing — and permitted — to share this information with you.

1.4 Right of First Refusal

So long as the Franchisee is not in default during the Term of this Agreement or any renewal hereof, the Franchisor will not enter into a franchise agreement with anyone other than the Franchisee for the operation of an additional EMMA & JEREMY'S Internet Café & Donut Emporium within the Protected Territory, nor will it operate any such operation on its own account unless in respect of each proposed additional EMMA & JEREMY'S Internet Café & Donut Emporium:

(a) The Franchisee has first given notice in writing to the Franchisor of the Franchisee's desire to establish such additional restaurant within the Protected Territory, in which case the proposed location therefore and the lease thereof to be taken by the Franchisor must both be approved in writing by the Franchisor in its sole discretion, and the Franchisor has then given notice in writing to the Franchisee offering the Franchisee the right to enter into a franchise agreement and sublease for such additional EMMA & JEREMY'S Internet Café & Donut Emporium in the Protected Territory in the Franchisor's then current form of franchise agreement and sublease (the terms and conditions of which may be substantially different from the terms of this Franchise Agreement and the sublease for the Franchised Location Premises specified herein);

(b) The Franchisor has first given notice in writing to the Franchisee of the Franchisor's intention to open an additional EMMA & JEREMY'S Internet Café & Donut Emporium in the Protected Territory and the Franchisor has offered the Franchisee the right to enter into a franchise agreement and sublease for such additional restaurant, both in the Franchisor's then current form;

(c) The Franchisee has not, within 7 days of receiving the notice referred to in Subsection 1.4(b), notified the Franchisor in writing that the Franchisee wishes to accept the offer contained in such notice.

(d) If the Franchisee does not accept the offer referred to in subsection 1.4(b), or otherwise fails to accept such offer in the time provided, then the Franchisor may either operate the additional EMMA & JEREMY'S Internet Café & Donut Emporium itself or enter into a franchise agreement in respect of the additional EMMA & JEREMY'S Internet Café & Donut Emporium with any other person, provided that the franchise agreement for such other person shall not contain terms and conditions substantially more favourable to the other person than those offered to the Franchisee.

Some agreements will grant you a five-kilometre protected territory but will also grant you a right of first refusal within that territory to develop another store if the franchisor determines that population and demographics justify another store in that area. If you are unable to exercise the right of first refusal or do not exercise it within the set time period prescribed in the agreement, then the franchisor is entitled to develop the location for itself, or license another party to enter into the territory. In other words, "Here's your big territory, and if you don't put a second location in it if we say so, then we will, and your territory is reduced accordingly." If this is the franchisor's business model, perhaps there is a way to soften the blow. There is sometimes room for negotiation on the extent of the territory and the timing for such right of first refusal (e.g., the franchisor shall not invoke this clause for the first 24 months of the term).

In any right of first refusal situation contemplated by section **1.4**, if you decline the opportunity to establish another location in what is supposed to be your exclusive territory, you would be wise to ensure that the franchisor does not make a more favourable offer to another franchisee without bringing that more favourable offer to you first. Saying, "I turned it down because it cost way too much" is fine until you learn that after you turned it down, the franchisor made major monetary concessions to establish the location with someone else. Perhaps the franchisor should not have the right to grant a franchise to another person on materially different terms without giving you the opportunity to make the same deal.

> If at any time during the Term the Franchisee is in material default under this Agreement pursuant to Article 11 or otherwise, then the right of first refusal provided for in this Section 1.4(a) shall thereafter be made available to the Franchisee only at the sole option of the Franchisor, which option the Franchisor may exercise in its absolute discretion.

In section **1.2**, the franchisor has granted an exclusive territory. This means a new franchised or corporate store can't be located within a five-kilometre radius of the premises. But the franchisor can ignore or reduce the protected territory if the franchisee is in default or the franchisor takes advantage of the right of first refusal provision in section **1.4**.

As discussed above, the real issue is sub-sections (b) through (d) of section **1.4**. Essentially, if the franchisor thinks the exclusive territory granted to you can support the establishment of another location, the franchisor can give notice to you that it wishes you to establish another location within your five-kilometre exclusive territory. If you fail to commit to establishing another franchise in your exclusive territory, then the franchisor can establish one either for itself or for another franchisee.

Some systems are well known for this; they require a successful franchisee to open another location within an exclusive territory, at a time not of the franchisee's choosing (with the risk of the second location cannibalizing the sales of the first location). So the franchisee must either establish this second location within his or her territory or face the franchisor (or another franchisee) a few blocks away.

Again, if the franchisor is adamant that this clause must remain in the agreement, try to secure an agreement that it won't be invoked for the first two or three years of the term. This would allow you to prepare for (and perhaps save for) the eventuality that you might have to open up a second location.

1.5   Reservation of Rights to the Franchisor

(a)   The Franchisor reserves the right to itself to market certain EMMA & JEREMY'S Internet Café & Donut Emporium products, including promotional or novelty items bearing the EMMA & JEREMY'S Internet Café & Donut Emporium Trade-marks through alternative channels of distribution that are not the same as or substantially similar to the franchised business, including through retail outlets of others within the Franchised Territory that are not conducted in the same or a substantially similar business format to the franchised business.

You should be aware of the clause that grants the franchisor a reserved right to distribute products or services through "alternative channels of distribution" within your protected territory. Effectively, this means that even though the franchisor may be somehow restricted from operating, licensing, or franchising a store within your protected territory, the franchisor is not barred from selling the product that is normally sold by you to retail department or food stores for inevitable sale to the public. Accordingly, you may discover, as the new owner of Emma & Jeremy's Internet Café & Donut Emporium with a five-kilometre protected or exclusive territory, that "frozen" Emma & Jeremy's Donuts are being sold in the frozen food section of the Safeway next door.

(b)   The Franchisor further reserves the right to itself to offer, or to licence the other of EMMA & JEREMY'S Internet Café & Donut Emporium products to the public anywhere through the conduct of a mail, telephone, or Internet order business, including the right to advertise, market, and otherwise promote the sale of such products through such mail, telephone, or Internet order business anywhere, including within the Franchised Territory.

Clause 1.5(b) allows a franchisor to sell product directly to consumers within your exclusive territory by mail, 1-800 number, or Internet. This means the consumers within your territory do not necessarily acquire the product from you, but rather they phone or email their orders into Chicago or Toronto for distribution by mail or some other form of delivery. I say necessarily, because the franchisor might not ship out of a centralized location. It may in fact refer such orders to the nearest franchisee to the customer! So it's not necessarily a bad thing; you just have to ask the franchisor what its policy is. It may in fact work well for you or it may not.

By means of this provision, the franchisor may also sell the products by way of corporate or national sales, which means the franchisor reserves the right to sell its products to "HIJ Company" or to one or more national accounts and all its stores or offices within the territory without involving the franchisee, which has rights to such territory. Or, as in our example above, it may refer these orders to the nearest franchisee to the customer. The nearest franchisee may (or may not) be you.

It's up to you (and your franchise lawyer) to assess what the franchisor's customary practice is for 1-800 orders, mail, or Internet orders and national accounts. If your territory in Victoria includes the downtown core where most government offices are located, and the franchise involves the sale of consumables that a large institution (such as a government) might wish to purchase, it's best to sort out the national accounts clause in advance.

(c)   The Franchisor may also acquire, develop, operate, licence, and franchise other types of retail locations which may involve the sale of similar products and services but which operate under different trade-marks and which may be located anywhere including nearby to the Franchised Location; provided that Franchisor will not itself initially develop, operate, licence, or franchise any such other retail locations which are located directly within the Franchised Territory, and if Franchisor should acquire any such other operating retail location, or the franchising rights to the same, which is located directly within the Franchised Territory, Franchisor will use its reasonable best efforts to achieve a solution to such situation which accommodates as best it reasonably can for the interests of all parties concerned, as soon as is reasonably practicable in the circumstances, and Franchisor shall incur no liability to Franchisee in connection therewith.

As discussed above, the reservation of rights provision noted above is reasonably standard, but nevertheless problematic for you if the franchisor decides to rely on it. If the franchisor decides to start selling frozen Emma & Jeremy's Donuts to Safeway, Loblaws, or other food outlets for retail distribution, chances are that such food outlet may be within your exclusive or protected territory (if you have one). The question is this: is a customer going to buy Emma & Jeremy's Donuts from your warm, cozy, and expensive location or is a customer going to purchase these products (perhaps frozen or prepackaged) at Safeway where they do their weekly run for groceries?

In these circumstances, Safeway's per unit price will be well below that charged or chargeable by you for the donuts (or the mix to make the donuts). This is because Safeway is so large it will get larger volume discounts. For customers, it may in fact be more convenient to buy frozen donuts from Safeway than to go to your warm and cozy franchised location. If it's cheaper and more convenient to go to Safeway, your sales may be cannibalized by the big grocery chain store next door.

If the franchisor is unwilling to strike this provision, the solution may be that the franchisor could be permitted to distribute any product it wants through grocery stores or by other alternate channels of distribution as long as it doesn't do so under the trade-mark used by you for the franchised business (or one that might be colourfully imitative or confusingly similar). That is, if it wants to distribute frozen donuts in Safeway under the name "Sennewald's Real German Donuts" it may do so, but it should not do so under the name "Emma & Jeremy's."

> (d)   Notwithstanding any other provision of this Agreement, Franchisor may itself or through an affiliate acquire, develop, operate, licence, or franchise any form of business anywhere which is not specifically granted, franchised, and licensed to Franchisee under this Agreement; and it may do so under the same, a similar or a different trade-mark; and any such form of business may be competitive with the franchised business but operate under a different trade-mark.

As discussed above, review your agreement for these provisions and discuss it with the franchisor, if you can, and your franchise lawyer as well. Ask if the franchisor is selling the same (or substantially the same) products in grocery stores. You should determine whether the franchisor is reserving the sale of all products to a large lucrative company that just happens to be in your exclusive territory.

It should be stated here that there is nothing necessarily improper about all this. Simply, you must be aware of the franchisor's "reserved rights" and the limited extent of the franchise being granted. If the very nature of the business is such that there is a risk of product being sold through department or food stores, mail order, telephone sales, or over the Internet, this is legitimately the subject of discussion and perhaps clarification between the parties. To the extent that the franchisor's actual or intended activities are not disclosed to you and reserved by the franchise agreement, or are otherwise unexpected, you may have a legitimate complaint against the franchisor for encroachment upon your exclusive territory.

1.6   Term and Effective Date

Unless otherwise specified in Schedule "A" to this Agreement or any addendum to this Agreement, the term of the franchise granted herein shall be FIVE (5) years from the date hereof (hereinafter called the "Term"). The Term shall begin on the effective date of this Agreement and unless sooner terminated as herein provided, shall expire FIVE (5) years thereafter. The effective date of this Agreement shall be the date set out in Schedule "A" to this Agreement, and the date upon which the Term commences. However, notwithstanding any other provision of this Agreement, or any sublease between the Franchisor and the Franchisee, in no event shall the Term of this franchise exceed the term under any lease or sublease for the Franchised Location, and this Agreement shall be construed accordingly.

Is the term being granted five years with an option to renew for an additional five? Or is it being granted for ten years with an option to renew for an additional period? "Five and five" seems to be the standard these days, although there are valid business reasons for shorter and longer terms from the perspective of the franchisor and the industry in which the franchisor is operating.

Five years seems to be the standard, mostly because the standard lease for a commercial mall tends to be five years. Franchisors do not normally want to (nor should they) grant franchises for longer than the term of the lease. (How can you operate the franchised business under the agreement if you have no lawful right to the premises past a particular date?) The above provision states that the term will not exceed the term under any lease, so if the franchise agreement is for a term of five years, but the lease has four years and six months left, the agreement will be deemed to expire when the lease expires, even though a previous section seemed to grant a full five years.

If the term was a ten-year term, it might not be to the client's advantage because if the business fails, then, subject to mitigation (the duty of the party not in breach to attempt to reduce damages the other party must bear), the potential damages that could accrue against you and your principals would be the value of the franchisor's bargain for a period of time, up to the balance of the term of the agreement.

Again, and subject to mitigation, a business failing in year three of a ten-year term, may have up to seven additional years of potential exposure whereas the failed business under a five-year arrangement would only have two years' potential exposure to concern itself with. A lawyer can assist you with these kinds of issues.

The term should also be "co-terminus" (i.e., running together) with the lease or sublease, so that the franchise does not expire at some point in time after the lease or sublease expires. This is very important to deal with if the lease or sublease has no renewal options.

1.7   Renewal

If upon expiry of the Term of this Agreement, the Franchisee is in compliance with all of the material terms and conditions of this Agreement, and only if the Franchisee has the right to remain in possession of the Franchised Location Premises for the length of the renewal term described below, then the Franchisee shall have the right to renew this Agreement for one further term of five (5) years, upon the following terms and conditions. The terms and conditions for each renewal of this Agreement are as follows:

Most renewal provisions are standard and more or less look like this one. (A renewal clause is sometimes referred to as a "New Franchise" or a "Subsequent Franchise.") You aren't entitled to a renewal term unless you are in compliance under your existing franchise and related agreements and are also in compliance with the franchisor's specific terms of renewal noted below in sections (a) through (g).

You must watch for clauses that are written to the effect that "the Franchisee shall be and shall continually have been in compliance under the franchise agreement" or words to that effect. The risk is that, if you have been in default once and have cured the default, you may still not be entitled to renewal because you were not "continually in compliance." Certainly, if you have been in default and have cured such default (such as a monetary default) then, subject to the other conditions of renewal, you should be considered to have always been in compliance. Although the franchisor won't like it, tinkering with the wording of the franchise agreement by negotiation with the franchisor may well be called for in this instance.

Since the 1980s, there have been more agreements that define specifically the conditions in which a franchisor is obligated to renew the franchise as opposed to the type of clause that granted you an option to renew if you were in "substantial compliance" under the franchise agreement.

You should consider the number of renewal terms contemplated by the franchise agreement, or whether the franchise agreement specifically expresses that you will be able to renew the franchise agreement for an unlimited number of successive renewal terms, dependent upon continued compliance. In franchises where the amount of investment by you and the ongoing business value of the franchised location are substantial, the length of time during which you may operate the business could be quite important. Banks may be reluctant to finance the business if there is not sufficient time in the term for you to recoup the investment.

Lastly, are the terms of renewal the terms you agreed to when the franchise agreement was signed four years ago, or are they the renewal terms in the franchisor's new form of agreement you're required to sign? Legally, it's likely that the renewal provisions in the existing agreement govern, not conditions that the franchisee has not agreed to in the renewal agreement. The conditions of renewal can be a moving target, and if they are, is there anything you can do about it? Try to ensure that the specific provisions negotiated for the initial term "carry over" for the renewal terms, or they will only last for the intial term.

(a)   The Franchisee shall notify the Franchisor in writing at least six (6) months prior to the expiry of the Term (or first renewal term, as the case may be), that it wishes to exercise its option to renew;

If you don't give notice to the franchisor of your intention to renew as and when required under the agreement (in this case, six months before the end of the term), it means you might well be deemed to have determined not to renew. The franchisor may find another operator for that location based upon you forgetting to formally renew. Always know the dates that you must give notice of your intent to renew, because if you forget it, you may well lose that right.

(b)   The Franchisee's option to renew shall only be effective if, at the time of its exercise and at the time of commencement of the renewal term, the Franchisee shall have fully complied with all of the material terms and conditions of this Agreement, and the Franchisee shall have the right to remain in possession of the Franchised Location Premises for the renewal term of five (5) years;

You must be in possession (by way of lease, sublease, or otherwise) of the franchised location premises for the renewal term (i.e., you can't have a new franchise term for five years if there is only six months left to run on the lease).

(c)   The Franchisee and any guarantor required by the Franchisor shall execute and deliver to the Franchisor a new Franchise Agreement for the renewal term in the Franchisor's then-current standard form, which may include terms and conditions which differ from those contained in this Agreement, including, but without limitation, the amount of Continuing Royalties and other fees and charges; to it.

The franchisee and any guarantors must execute the franchisor's then current standard form of franchise agreement. Franchise agreements are always being changed by lawyers to keep abreast with changing laws and market circumstances. This is normal. New developments in the law will cause the franchisor to modify its agreement every few years so that it is up to date and the franchisor's interests are protected. Be assured that today's franchise agreement will be different than the franchise agreement you look at in five years time.

If negotiation is possible on this point (which is not at all certain), perhaps the best that you could hope for is an assurance that the royalty rates and advertising fund contributions do not rise from those contained in the original franchise agreement. Or that the material financial obligations of you under the new franchise agreement will not differ substantially from those contained in the original franchise agreement.

> (d)   The Franchisee and all individuals who have signed this Agreement in their personal capacities, shall, at the option of the Franchisor, execute a release of any claims it and they may have against the Franchisor and its directors and officers, in a form satisfactory to the Franchisor's solicitors; and

It's quite normal for the franchisor to require the franchisee and guarantors to release the franchisor and its directors and officers from all liabilities in respect of the expiring term. In fairness to the franchisor, why would the franchisor renew your term for five more years if you are going to sue the franchisor for something that may have happened during the previous term? So if there are legal issues that are "actionable" by you, those legal issues become moot (i.e., game over) upon release by you and renewal by the franchisor.

The release of the franchisor for the previous term is standard, but if possible, it should be mutual, such that both parties release each other from any claims or actions in respect of the first or previous term of the franchise agreement. (What is sauce for the goose is sauce for the gander!)

> (e)   The Franchisee shall carry out the Franchisor's required upgrading, replacements, repairs, and improvements to the Franchised Location and Franchised Business and the equipment used therein in order to conform to the Franchisor's then-current image, standards, and specifications.

If refurbishment or redecoration is required as a condition of renewal, it might be prudent to cap the amount of money the franchisor expects you to pay for refurbishment. Capping any open-ended expense is prudent where possible, although to be fair, it is not always possible for the franchisor to do this if it is unsure what a renovation might look like, let alone cost in five years.

With respect to capital expenditures, a clause such as the one referred to above is standard but you must be careful that such capital expenditures are not imposed against you in differing circumstances and at different times throughout the term. For instance, there could be a similar provision within the sublease or the lease that calls for refurbishment at a different time in the term. You could be faced with refurbishment as directed by the landlord under the lease or sublease, and refurbishment at the conclusion of the franchise agreement term as directed by the franchisor as a condition of renewal.

Moreover, the "system change" clause (see section **1.8** below), which is normal in franchise agreements, may also impose, by necessity, a requirement for capital expenditures for refurbishment. Perhaps an agreement can be secured to the effect that any refurbishment required under the franchise agreement, or any of the other agreements, if at all, will be coordinated, and will be scheduled at the time of renewal, or only at certain defined intervals during the franchise term.

The requirement to make changes is not necessarily a bad thing, you just need to be aware of it so that you can plan for it and ensure that costs stay within some semblance of order. Franchise systems are always undergoing change to keep up with the times and the fickle and changing tastes of customers, and I suppose, fickle and changing customers. You need only to look in McDonald's restaurants every two or three years to see differing colour schemes and décor, and different offerings. The Keg franchise has undergone a similar design change from its ski cabin/railway station motifs from the 1970s. Other franchises that have not kept up with the times may still look like they originally did in the 1970s, with potentially negative business results (unless of course you happen to like the '70s).

> (f)   The Franchisee acknowledges that the Franchisor will incur expenses in connection with any renewal, and thus the Franchisee shall reimburse the Franchisor for its reasonable actual expenses incurred in connection with the renewal and shall pay to the Franchisor a Renewal Fee; the payment of which shall be a condition of the Franchisor granting consent to the renewal; and

As of 2009, the franchisor will incur costs in respect of the renewal, in particular, legal fees of between $1,500 and $2,500 (depending upon the lawyer, the firm, and the city the lawyer has his or her practice). If possible, these costs should be capped. Note that the words "reasonable legal fees and expenses" will assist if the franchisor is unwilling to cap this cost. Sometimes the franchisor will charge a renewal fee in addition to the recapture of legal costs referred to above. It isn't unusual for the cost to be between $5,000 and $10,000 (or a percentage of the then current initial franchise fee). It is a business decision you must make as to whether it's worth it for you to have to pay a fee for renewal as well as the franchisor's legal expenses for renewal.

Perhaps a clause whereby the franchisee must pay all the franchisor's administrative and legal costs respecting a renewal could be capped (e.g., no greater than $2,000).

> (g)   This option to renew shall be null and void if the Franchisee has no right (by way of lease or sub-lease) to remain in possession of the Franchise Location Premises.

1.8   System Change

> The Franchisor shall have the right to make changes, modifications, or additions to the EMMA & JEREMY'S System as described herein from time to time by reasonable notice in

writing to the Franchisee. The Franchisee acknowledges that some of such changes may be material and may involve required expenditures due to the addition or substitution of new food or other products, services, inventory, supplies, food preparation and cooking equipment, other equipment or technology, or an alteration of specifications or standards or an alteration or modification of the trade-marks. Upon receipt of notice from the Franchisor, the Franchisee agrees to comply with and carry out all such changes, modifications, and additions, and to undertake and satisfactorily complete any additional training requirements, at its own expense, within the time reasonably specified by such notice, as if they were a part of the EMMA & JEREMY'S System at the time of execution of this Agreement.

This is the system change clause of the type that you'll find in many franchise agreements in Canada. This clause allows a franchisor to modify or alter the "system" during the term, with you bearing your own expenses for the modifications or additions.

It purports to allow the franchisor to change the system if it determines that the system needs to react to changes in the market or to new technologies. For example, head office at Emma & Jeremy's decides they want to introduce pizza in addition to donuts. Although the introduction of pizza to the Emma and Jeremy's system might catch more of a lunch crowd and therefore might well be a rational business decision, it could cost you, as the franchisee, a lot of money. Pizza is cooked in a pizza oven, and the introduction of pizza ovens might be a very expensive undertaking by you because you would have to pay for the oven, not to mention having to deal with space issues, electrical upgrades, and perhaps lease issues (e.g., your landlord may already have a pizza outlet in his or her mall and is contractually obligated to prevent another pizza restaurant from operating at that mall). So the introduction of pizza ovens might well be justified under this clause or perhaps it is a poorly thought out idea that will cost too much money.

"I bought an Internet café and donut shop, not a pizza factory," might be the response of a skeptical franchisee. Another franchisee may be upset because his or her landlord won't allow the sale of pizza. Or another response by a franchisee may be, "I have no venting in my space for cooking odours and it's not wired for 220 volts." So a change in the fundamental terms of the agreement might open up a hornet's nest of problems and may not be justifiable under this clause.

A more extreme example might well be the "Jack-in-the Box" concept from the United States, which discovered many years ago that its "clown" concept was not working. Television commercials were run "blowing up" the clown mascot and Jack in the Box carried on without the clown in its advertising for a number of years. This may have involved other system changes at the same time, such as new menus, new decor, capital alterations, etc., for the franchisees. But in that case, the franchisor had determined that this one aspect of its system was not well received in the marketplace and for the benefit of the entire franchised system, it disposed of that element (with a bang). (Ironically, the clown was re-introduced to their advertising some years later.)

If a system remains stagnant, it eventually withers on the vine and for the benefit of the entire system, the franchisor ought to be in the position of directing where the system goes and how it develops. System change clauses are, accordingly, standard. However, system change clauses should not be invoked by a franchisor for changes it is not prepared to undergo in its own corporate stores. System change requirements should be based upon achieving and maintaining uniformity throughout the franchise system.

This system change clause might also allow the franchisor to change trademarks, which is perhaps a justifiable objective in an evolving market (e.g., Bend-off-Versterr became IKON). But what if the franchisor doesn't have a registered trade-mark at the time the franchise agreement is entered, and chooses to rely on the system change clause to pass the expense of re-branding on to the franchisee? The answer is to assess the trade-mark status of the franchisor before the contract is entered, and if there is no registered mark, then to allocate costs of re-branding (e.g., signage replacement) in the event the mark is unregistrable. See Chapter 10 for more discussion on trade-mark issues.

1.9 Owner-Operator

The Franchisee acknowledges that the Franchisor has granted this Franchise on the material representation of the Franchisee and the Guarantor that the person(s) designated in Schedule "A" to this Agreement are "owner-operators" and shall participate actively on a full-time and best efforts basis in the management and operation of the Franchised Business.

The "full time best efforts clause" means just that; you must devote your full time and best efforts to running the business. Buying and operating another business "on the side" may well breach this clause, and may also breach the in term restrictive covenant contained in the franchise agreement if the businesses are similar.

Justifiably, many franchisors want the person with whom they originally contracted to be owner-operator; they do not want absentee franchisees who simply hire managers to run the business.

If you intend to run the business through managers, you might well be advised to negotiate this provision and obtain the franchisor's consent.

6

TENANCY AND DEVELOPMENT

2. TENANCY AND DEVELOPMENT

2.1 Sublease Of Franchised Location Premises from the Franchisor

If the Franchisor (or its affiliate) leases the Franchised Location Premises directly from the landlord of such premises, then the Franchisee shall sublease the premises from the Franchisor (or its affiliates) and shall forthwith upon request by the Franchisor execute a Sublease substantially in accordance with the Franchisor's then-current standard form of Sublease, and the Franchisee shall duly and timely make all required payments under and perform and observe all terms, provisions, covenants, conditions, and obligations contained in such Sublease as if they were incorporated into and formed a part of this Agreement. Subject to section 2.4 herein, the Franchisee shall not enter into possession of the Franchised Location Premises unless and until the Franchisee has executed and delivered the Franchisor's form of Sublease, which will be required to be guaranteed by the Guarantor. Failure by the Franchisee and the Guarantor to execute and deliver the Sublease to the Franchisor within five (5) days after a written request shall constitute a default under and a material breach of this Agreement entitling the Franchisor to terminate this Agreement forthwith. Any payments made or credits given by the head landlord of the Franchised Location Premises to induce the Franchisor to establish, construct, and develop the Franchised Location Premises as an EMMA & JEREMY'S Internet Café & Donut Emporium (including, but without limitation, tenant inducements) may be retained by the Franchisor in whole or in part at its sole discretion.

The tenancy/development provisions can be complicated, and if not understood, can cost you a lot of money. Franchise lawyers can assist in helping you understand these provisions.

There are three ways you can secure premises for the franchised business:

- You own the real estate.

- You have a lease directly with the landlord unrelated to the franchisor.

- You have acquired the premises by way of a sublease from the franchisor itself, which means the franchisor has already entered a head lease with the landlord and has the right to sublease the premises to you.

Franchisors normally like to control the location of the franchisee's business by way of subleases. If the franchisor has a sublease with you, then it will be easier for the franchisor to "take control" of that location (i.e., take it over and evict you) should you default under the sublease (e.g., by not paying rent). (A default under the franchise agreement will normally be a default under the sublease entitling the franchisor to treat the default as if it were a commercial tenancy dispute. This is referred to as "cross default.") Should you default under these circumstances, the franchisor can take advantage of remedies that would not normally be available if the franchisor wasn't also one of the sub-landlords.

If you are not a successful franchise operator and either "walk away" from the business or are terminated, then this creates a big and expensive problem for the franchisor if the franchisor is also the sub-landlord under the head lease: It's on the hook for the rent you would have to have paid for the balance of the term of the lease. In large established systems, this may not be the end of the world; the store might be operated corporately for a few months until a new franchisee is found for that location (with a new franchise fee being paid). But in other systems, the franchisor might not have the financial or human resources to operate the failed franchised outlet let alone the financial resources to pay the rent. So for the franchisor, there's a lot riding on your success, and it's a risk assessment.

Rent has to be paid, and under a sublease, it's almost always paid by the subtenant-franchisee directly to the landlord. The franchise agreement and sublease may provide that rent under the sublease is to be paid directly to the franchisor; the idea being that the franchisor will send the cheque through its account and immediately pay the landlord.

In recessionary times (or in a system having financial problems), some franchisors have been known to retain rent money destined for a third party landlord; the franchisee discovering the hard way that his or her rent cheque for the last two months was cashed, but the franchisor used it for its own purposes and didn't pay the landlord. For these reasons, I like franchisees to pay rent to the landlord directly.

Another question to ask yourself when you are dealing with a sublease would be: Is the franchisor up-charging on the rent? That is, is the franchisor sub-landlord being charged $2,000 per month for all rent and operating costs, but is charging you, as the subtenant franchisee, $2,500 per month? Maybe for a good location an up-charge similar to this is justifiable. And then again, maybe it isn't. Certainly these matters would be material enough to require disclosure in those Canadian jurisdictions in which disclosure is required.

You should also inquire whether or not the franchisor is receiving any "tenant inducement money" or "TI" money in respect to securing the franchised location or entering into the head lease with the landlord. Tenant inducements are payments made by landlords to the franchisor directly, or other compensation the franchisor receives in terms of construction and other matters for developing the premises. In most cases, the money is directed into the construction and development of the premises. It is up to you to make the inquiry regarding whether the franchisor is receiving any TI money, how much the franchisor is receiving, and where the TI money is going.

In some cases, the franchisor does not disclose to the franchisee the amount of tenant inducement money it receives. Although there may be some justification for the franchisor taking some of the inducement monies to compensate it for the risks associated with "being on the hook" for the lease and the construction contract, the amount of those inducements should be disclosed to you. It's suggested here that a 50/50 split of the inducements may not be unreasonable. Keeping the inducements without disclosure is unreasonable.

2.2   Lease of Franchised Location Premises Directly by the Franchisee

(a)   If the Franchisee leases the Franchised Location Premises directly from a landlord of such Premises, it shall do so only with the prior written consent of the Franchisor, and the Franchisee agrees that it will not enter into any offer to lease or lease for the Franchised Location Premises until it shall first have submitted the proposed offer to lease or lease to the Franchisor and the Franchisor shall have given its written approval of the terms and conditions of the proposed offer to lease or lease, such approval not to be unreasonably or arbitrarily withheld or delayed;

(b)   The Franchisor may request that the Lease contain terms satisfactory to the Franchisor to protect the Franchisor's third party beneficial interest in the Franchised Location Premises as an operating EMMA & JEREMY'S Internet Café & Donut Emporium, such as an agreement to the effect that the landlord will agree not to lease any other premises in the same development to a donut shop or an Internet café concept;

(c)   That the landlord will agree to notify the Franchisor in the event of any breach or default of the Lease by the Franchisee, or any failure by the Franchisee to exercise a right of renewal of the Lease, or any application by the Franchisee for consent to assign or sublet the Lease, and that the landlord will allow the Franchisor the right to cure the breach or default or exercise any right of renewal in the place and instead of the Franchisee and to succeed to the rights of the Franchisee as the Lessee under the Lease, or to also give its consent to the proposed assignment or subletting;

(d)   That the landlord will recognize an assignment of the Lease from the Franchisee to the Franchisor carried out pursuant to the terms of this Franchise Agreement;

(e)   The Franchisee shall not assign or sublet the Lease during the term of this Agreement without first offering the assignment or subletting to the Franchisor and if the Franchisor shall not accept the assignment or subletting to itself within ten (10) days, then the Franchisee may only assign or sublet the lease with the prior written consent of the Franchisor, such consent not to be unreasonably or arbitrarily withheld or delayed;

(f)   Any monies expended by the Franchisor to cure a breach or default or to pay any arrears owing by the Franchisee under the Lease shall be deemed to be additional sums due to the Franchisor hereunder and shall be paid by the Franchisee to the Franchisor immediately upon demand; and

(g)   The Franchisee agrees that the Franchisor may negotiate directly with the Landlord in respect of the above matters, and that if the landlord enters into an agreement for the aforesaid purposes with the Franchisor, then the Franchisee shall also enter into and execute the said agreement with the landlord and the Franchisor.

Regarding the tenancy arrangement, the franchisor has two usual options. One is to lease the premises directly from a third party landlord and sublet those premises to you under a sublease. The other option is to allow you to directly lease from a third party landlord, but often requiring the third party landlord to execute a form of "consent and waiver" or "tripartite" agreement. The consent and waiver or tripartite agreement gives the franchisor certain rights to cure the defaults of the franchisee/subtenant or to take over the premises in the event of default, or a failure to renew.

If the franchisor decides to allow you to enter into your own lease with the landlord, it might be only on terms acceptable to the franchisor. The lease might also be subject to the franchisor's approval.

Although I have spent innumerable hours attempting to negotiate these sorts of agreements with landlords, in my experience, landlords are reluctant to entertain tripartite agreements giving the franchisor "special treatment" in the event of a franchisee's default unless the franchisor is prepared to bite the bullet and go on the lease as a party and therefore be responsible for the obligations of the franchisee (or otherwise give the landlord a corporate guarantee).

The reason for the differing options is the balance between control and liability. If the franchisor leases the premises itself from the landlord, and does so for many locations, its liability exposure may be high. However, if the franchisor controls the location, a default under the franchise agreement can, through cross default wording, be a default under the sublease entitling the franchisor sub-landlord to terminate not only the franchise agreement but the sublease as well. What might have been a complicated lawsuit over franchisee non-performance and franchisee royalty withholding becomes very easily characterized as a commercial tenancy dispute in which the sub-landlord (franchisor) has simply not been paid additional rent. Certainly, it is much less complicated from a legal perspective for a sub-landlord to take back its premises than for a franchisor (who has no tenancy relationship with the franchisee tenant) to attempt to do the same. Many franchisors, however, do not necessarily want the exposure created by being the direct tenant on numerous leases, as stated above.

2.3 Development of Franchised Location Premises by the Franchisee

Normally, the Franchisor will construct, develop, and equip the Franchised Location Premises itself pursuant to Section 2.5 herein. However, if the Franchisor so directs in writing, the Franchisee shall be responsible for the development of the Franchised Location Premises according to the Franchisor's standard sample plans, specifications, layout, and design; the details of which shall be provided to the Franchisee. In such circumstance, the Franchisee shall be responsible for all costs associated in any way with such development. It shall be the Franchisee's responsibility to have prepared all specific construction plans and specifications to suit the shape and dimensions of the Franchised Location Premises based on the Franchisor's standard sample plans and specifications, as the Franchisor's sample plans are general in nature and provided for guidance only. The Franchisee must ensure that its construction plans and specifications comply with all applicable ordinances, building codes, fire department, and other permit requirements and with lease or sublease requirements and restrictions. At the Franchisee's complete expense, the Franchisee must obtain a development permit and building permit to develop the Franchised Location Premises within any reasonable time prescribed by the Franchisor. Additionally, it shall also be the Franchisee's responsibility under this Section 2.3 to:

(a)   Obtain all required occupancy, utility, health, sign, and business permits and licenses and any other required permits and licenses;

(b)   Construct all required improvements to the Franchised Location Premises and to decorate the Franchised Location in compliance with the Franchisor's standards and specifications (including colour scheme);

(c)   Obtain and install all equipment required by the Franchisor for use in EMMA & JEREMY'S Internet Café & Donut Emporium, including such equipment as may be necessary to store and dispose of all cooking oil and/or food products as required by law; and

(d)   Obtain and install all other furnishings and signs as required by the Franchisor for the EMMA & JEREMY'S Internet Café & Donut Emporium including indoor and/or outdoor illuminated signage (as the case may be).

If the Franchised Location Premises are developed by the Franchisee pursuant to this Section 2.3, the Franchisor has the right to inspect the construction and development of the Franchised Location Premises from time to time to ensure the Franchisee is in compliance with its obligations hereunder. If the Franchised Location Premises are abandoned by the Franchisee, or if the development of the Franchised Location Premises cannot, in the reasonable opinion of the Franchisor, be completed by the Franchisee, or if the development of the Franchised Location Premises cannot be completed in a timely manner or pursuant to the Franchisee's development schedule owing to factors including the Franchisee's inability or unwillingness to pay for such development, then the Franchisor, acting reasonably, may terminate this Franchise Agreement and any other agreement between the parties.

You can acquire the franchised businesses in a number of ways. You can buy the business from an existing operator or acquire it from the franchisor. If you acquire it from the franchisor, either the franchisor will be constructing and developing the premises (building it out and equipping it on a turnkey basis) or you will be responsible for construction and development of the premises according to the franchisor's specifications.

If the premises have not yet been developed, this could be an extremely problematic area if you are an inexperienced franchisee. If the premises are being developed by the franchisor or its contractors, there should be some assurances that costs will not exceed a set amount. If you have budgeted for construction of premises and leasehold improvements, at, for example, $180,000, you will start off your franchising relationship in extreme hardship if the costs actually come out to $260,000. You should try to negotiate fixed price contracts where possible.

2.4   Requirements of Opening of Franchised Location where Franchisee has Developed Premises

If the Franchised Location Premises are developed by the Franchisee pursuant to Section 2.3 herein, the Franchisee shall promptly complete all work, which is the responsibility of the Franchisee, and have all requirements attended to so that the Franchised Location Premises shall be open for business as promptly as is practicable after the execution of this Agreement.

The Franchised Location Premises shall not be opened without the prior written approval of the Franchisor, which approval shall not be unreasonably withheld. The Franchisee shall open the Franchised Location Premises for business and commence the conduct of its business within five days after the Franchisor's determination that the Franchised Location is in suitable condition therefore and that the Franchisee and its staff have been successfully trained according to the EMMA & JEREMY'S standards for training.

2.5 Development of the Franchised Location Premises by the Franchisor

If the Franchisor determines that it shall develop the Franchised Location Premises itself, then the following provisions will apply:

(a)   The Franchisor shall construct and develop the Franchised Location Premises on a turnkey basis for and on behalf of and at the sole cost and expense of the Franchisee;

Many franchisees do not have construction and contracting experience and accordingly leave it to the franchisor to build out the premises, stock the shelves, and order and install all the equipment. But does the franchisor have experience performing these functions, and what happens if there are cost overruns? The franchisor could be mistaken as to the estimated cost for the construction and development of the franchised location premises. Should that be for the franchisee to bear?

If the franchisor passes the invoice on to you expecting payment, what are you to do if you learn that the franchised business is costing 25 percent more than what the franchisor's estimate was. ("Oops!" might be a somewhat unsatisfactory response!) It is for that reason that you should attempt to "pin down" as much as possible the costs of construction and development.

If the franchisor has experience in building and developing franchised premises (the larger and more experienced ones always do) then the franchisor should be able to determine within a few thousand dollars, the total cost to develop, construct, and equip the franchised premises. Perhaps you are in a position to agree to the franchisor's estimate; however, if the actual cost exceeds the estimate by any more than say 5 to 10 percent, then any overruns of 5 to 10 percent above the estimate could be the franchisor's responsibility. This could be negotiated and concluded at the same time the franchise agreement is negotiated. Don't forget that there will be GST and PST that will be added to the inevitable bill you receive.

(b)   The Franchisor shall supply the working drawings and retain a general contractor or subcontractors of the Franchisor's choice to develop the Franchised Location Premises for and on behalf of the Franchisee in a good and workmanlike manner and at a total cost which the Franchisor determines to be reasonable in the circumstances. Such general contractor or subcontractors may be affiliates of the Franchisor, and shall be entitled to earn a reasonable profit from its (or their) engagement;

(c)   The Franchisee shall pay the full cost of construction and development of the Franchised Location, including the cost of such of the following items as are applicable:

Some of these costs may be costs that the franchisor does not pay to others but performs itself. The franchisor will normally attempt to pass on all or most of its costs relating to the acquisition and development of the premises. Are any of the costs being passed on "internal" costs such as internal salaries, or are all of these costs invoiced by third parties and payable by the franchisor? If internal administrative or salary costs are being passed on, there may be some opportunity of negotiating this point. (Should you be paying for someone who is already on the franchisor's payroll?)

(i)   Searching for and selecting the Franchised Location;

(ii)   the cost of any leasing commissions paid to secure the Franchised Location;

(iii)   the cost of preparing the site plan for the Franchised Location;

(iv)   the cost of negotiating the offer to lease and the lease, and preparing the sublease;

(v)   the cost of obtaining the consent of the landlord to the sublease;

(vi)   where required by the landlord or the Franchisor, the cost of registration of the lease, and where applicable, the sublease, at the appropriate Land Title Office, including all taxes, legal fees, and disbursements that may be payable in connection therewith;

(vii)   the costs of obtaining all required regulatory and other approvals, including development permits, building permits, health permits, and landlord approval;

(viii) the cost of preparing the plans and specifications for the interior and exterior design and layout, and the construction working drawings;

(ix) all reasonable and prudent costs of insurance and bonding in connection with the construction and development of the Franchised Location Premises;

(x) all costs of designing and constructing the leasehold improvements and acquiring, delivering, and installing the furnishings, equipment, fixtures, signs, and initial supplies and inventory;

(xi) all costs of providing for and obtaining all required utilities and other service hook ups; and

(xii) any other direct costs incurred by the Franchisor in respect of the construction and development of the Franchised Location.

(d) The Franchisor shall advise the Franchisee of all such estimated and actual costs and fees from time to time as and when they are estimated and ascertained;

(e) The Franchisee shall pay to the Franchisor upon request a deposit and one or more advances against the estimated or actual costs and fees to be incurred and charged by the Franchisor in constructing and developing the Franchised Location Premises. The Franchisee shall pay the Franchisor's said costs and fees from time to time in accordance with Schedule "A" attached hereto. The Franchisor will invoice the Franchisee for all of the aforesaid costs and fees from time to time, and all such invoices shall be paid in full by the Franchisee immediately upon receipt;

(f) The Franchisor reserves the right to require payment by the Franchisee of all such costs and fees invoiced to date prior to giving possession of the Franchised Location to the Franchisee to commence business;

It is normal for the franchisor to want to be fully paid for construction and development prior to allowing you to open for business.

(g) The Franchisor and the Franchisee shall also reasonably agree in writing that the Franchised Location has been substantially completed by the Franchisor and is ready for delivery of possession to the Franchisee to commence business, prior to the Franchisor so delivering possession;

(h) The Franchisor shall, upon the Franchisee's written request, deliver evidence of title to the leasehold improvements, furnishings, fixtures, equipment, signs, supplies, and inventory (other than leased items) to the Franchisee by a bill of sale or other appropriate title document upon receiving payment in full for all of the costs and fees incurred and charged by the Franchisor in connection therewith. However, no bill of sale is required to be provided if the Franchisor has not been paid in full for such items. When the Franchisor has been paid in full, title shall pass to the Franchisee free and clear of all liens, charges, and encumbrances;

You should obtain a bill of sale or some evidence of title to the equipment you are buying from the franchisor or its suppliers. If the franchisor or its suppliers have not been fully paid in respect to this equipment, the franchisor should be under no obligation to provide a bill of sale on items it has not been paid for.

If you are not sure if you are acquiring the equipment "free and clear," you can have your lawyer perform a personal property security search or related search to assess whether the seller/supplier of that item has a charge or lien against it. Liens should be released and discharged upon payment of the money.

(i)   In respect of leased items for the Franchised Location Premises, the Franchisor shall either (and at its choice) assign the leases for such items to the Franchisee, who shall then assume all obligations thereunder and indemnify the Franchisor in respect thereof. Or the Franchisee may direct the Franchisee to enter into such leases itself directly with the suppliers of such items. Or the Franchisee may retain the leases in the Franchisor's own name and invoice the Franchisee from time to time for all payments required to be made thereunder, in which case the Franchisee shall make all such payments promptly as invoiced; and

(j)   A list of the furnishings, fixtures, equipment, signs, and initial supplies and inventory to be installed at the Franchised Location Premises is attached as part of Schedule "A" hereto or will be added to Schedule "A" hereto as soon as the same has been settled by the Franchisor.

Is the franchisor providing any warranty on the equipment that is being sold to you? Or must you go to the manufacturer directly in respect of warranty work? Is the franchisor equipping the premises with the same standard of equipment that it originally agreed to, or is "less expensive" or second hand equipment being used instead? If second hand equipment or lesser quality equipment has been agreed to by you and the franchisor in advance, then this is not an issue. However, if you believe that you are getting brand new first-rate quality equipment (e.g., refrigeration equipment, ovens, etc.) complete with warranty, and you are getting used equipment (without warranty), then there is a potential legal issue that might affect the future of the relationship. Clarify this at the outset.

7

PRODUCTS AND SUPPLIES

3. REQUIRED PRODUCTS AND SUPPLIES FOR AN EMMA & JEREMY'S INTERNET CAFÉ & DONUT EMPORIUM

3.1 Required Purchase and Use of Equipment and Signs

The Franchisee shall lease and install all signs and displays required by the Franchisor for use in operation of the Franchised Business only from the Franchisor or from suppliers designated or approved by the Franchisor from time to time. If signs or other equipment are required for use in the operation of the Franchised Business are to be leased from the Franchisor, then the Franchisee shall execute and deliver to the Franchisor on request, the Franchisor's standard form of sign or equipment lease, as the case may be. In such circumstances, the Franchisee acknowledges and agrees that a default under this Franchise Agreement is a default under the sign or equipment lease, as the case may be, and a default under the sign lease is a default under this Franchise Agreement, entitling the Franchisor to remove from the Franchised Location Premises any signage, equipment, or displays so leased, and take such other steps as provided for in this Agreement in circumstances where the Franchisee is in default.

It is standard in franchising that the franchisor will require you to purchase all equipment, supplies, and inventory being used in the business either directly from the franchisor, or from the franchisor's designated or approved suppliers. This is to ensure quality control, to create a large buying group so that the group can take advantage of volume discounts, and may also be used as a profit centre for the franchisor that may in fact have an ownership interest in the major supplier. There is nothing untoward or wrong in the franchisor requiring you to buy from it; the question is, what if the same products and services are available from another supplier at a far lesser cost? What if the franchisor cannot sell products less expensively than, for example, Costco?

It's bound to create some tension in the system if the franchisor insists franchisees buy from it or its suppliers. (For more information about approved suppliers, see section 3.4.)

Can the franchisor allow you to purchase products or supplies from alternative suppliers in circumstances in which the franchisor or its suppliers are not competitive as to pricing, or will this affect other prices charged to it and you? If you are able to acquire products or services of comparable quality at comparable or better prices from Save-On-Foods, Costco, or other large, low-cost retailers, the franchisor has both a practical and a legal problem. Although the franchisor may be entitled to default and perhaps terminate you for buying unauthorized products or services from unauthorized sources, other franchisees in the system are unlikely to be co-operative and happy if they too are being forced into buying product that is either too highly priced in the first instance, or artificially marked up by the franchisor. If the franchisees can get the same product elsewhere at less cost, they inevitably will.

3.2 Software Program(s) and Designated Hardware

If directed by the Franchisor, the Franchisee shall also license or sublicense (as the case may be) from the Franchisor (or its designated supplier), a POS, inventory control, and tracking software system, which may include software and certain hardware elements. The Franchisee shall execute and deliver to the Franchisor on request, the form of licensing or sublicensing agreement acceptable to the Franchisor and to the licensor of such program at the cost specified in such license, which the Franchisee agrees to pay pursuant to the terms of such computer system license. The Franchisee acknowledges and agrees that a default under this Franchise Agreement is a default under the computer system license and a default under the computer system license is a default under this Franchise Agreement, entitling the Franchisor (or the licensor of such hardware and software) to remove or render unusable any such hardware and software so licensed. The Franchisee agrees that the terms of such computer system license may require the Franchisee to pay for hardware and software, and to pay regularly for updates to the software.

As a franchise lawyer, I love this clause. The franchisor doesn't need to bring legal action against you for breaching the agreement; it simply has the legal right to turn off or render unusable inventory management, accounting, or other software that you need in order to run the business. It's a self-help remedy that brings faster results than court.

3.3 Equipment Leases

If it is desirable or necessary for any restaurant equipment situated at the Franchised Location Premises to be subject to an equipment lease, then the Franchisee may lease such equipment on terms and conditions acceptable to it, provided that the equipment so leased conforms with the Franchisor's standards and the Franchisee has obtained the Franchisor's prior written consent to such leasing, not to be unreasonably withheld.

3.4   Approved Suppliers

The Franchisee shall only purchase from the Franchisor or from suppliers designated or approved by the Franchisor from time to time, all goods and supplies used in the operation of an EMMA & JEREMY'S Internet Café & Donut Emporium including, but without limitation, the Franchisee's inventory of food supplies and other products used at or sold from the Franchised Business.

As noted above, the franchisor will require you to purchase all equipment, supplies, and inventory being used in the business either directly from the franchisor or from the franchisor's designated or approved supplier.

The reason for this is twofold. The franchisor wishes to ensure that quality will be the same throughout the system. If franchisees are entitled to purchase products, supplies, and inventory from a variety of sources, then some locations may use equipment, inventory, or supplies of a lesser quality, or may end up selling to the public products and services of a lesser quality than the franchisor requires.

The franchisor may be able to secure a better price on equipment, supplies, and inventory for it and its franchisees when it is part of a large organization. The cost per unit of supplies, equipment, and inventory may well be cheaper for you when you are part of the franchisor's buying group. Normally, the price will always be better than what you could do on your own account. In other worlds, the franchisor may have struck a better deal with a food or product or equipment supplier than you could ever obtain on your own because the franchisor is buying in bulk and is passing its savings on to you and the other franchisees in the system.

You should be aware that sometimes the supplier of a product or service is in fact the franchisor or one of its affiliated companies. (For example, a pancake franchisor might also own the company that supplies all the pancake mix and syrup.)

Although it is commonplace for you to purchase products or services from a franchisor or its designated or approved suppliers, what happens when you can purchase identical products or services at Costco or Wal-Mart for a cheaper price than is being offered by the franchisor or its suppliers?

In fairness to the franchisor, be aware that it may be able to provide a substantial savings on a host of other products and services you must use, but cannot change the price of that one item that sells 30 percent below cost at Wal-Mart.

Will the franchisor allow you to purchase products or supplies from alternative suppliers in circumstances in which the franchisor or its suppliers are not competitive as to pricing? Some franchisors may allow you to purchase supplies from an alternative supplier as long as such product meets the franchisor's standards and specifications (i.e., it is not inferior) and for a finite period of time until the franchisor's own product becomes either more readily available or more competitively priced. This may be something that can be discussed between you and the franchisor.

3.5   Allowances to the Franchisor

The Franchisee hereby acknowledges and agrees that the Franchisor shall be entitled to the benefit of any of all volume rebates, allowances, and other similar receipts and advantages that the Franchisor may obtain from any supplier by reason of such supplier supplying products or services to the Franchisor, the Franchisee and/or to other Franchisees of the Franchisor. For purposes of this Agreement, any landlord of the Franchisor is deemed to be a supplier.

The franchisor is entitled to any rebates that it receives from suppliers. Rebates or allowances are normal in business relationships in which a buyer is purchasing large quantities of product or services. This can either be reflected in a lesser price for the product or service, or the buyer receiving a rebate every quarter or every year (i.e., for every 15 cases of cola, the distributor sends the franchisor the 16th case for free). When these rebates amount to money, the question is, who gets it? Some franchisors take all of their rebates and "roll them back" into the franchised business through underwriting conventions or the advertising fund. Others keep all of the rebates and use it as a profit centre. This is a topic to discuss with the franchisor.

Franchise agreements will normally disclose that the franchisor or its designated or approved supplier is entitled to any benefits conferred upon it by wholesalers or manufacturers. Successful franchisors will endeavour to pass some or all of those benefits on to the franchisees directly or indirectly.

From a practical perspective, if you are able to buy product from the franchisor or its designated or approved supplier at considerably lower prices than you would if you were forced to buy as a solitary businessperson, you are not likely to raise this issue with the franchisor.

3.6   Payment Irregularities

In the event of any payment irregularities by the Franchisee, the Franchisor reserves the right to place the Franchisee or to request any approved supplier to place the Franchisee on a "no further delivery," "cash on delivery," or "prepaid" basis for future purchases of supplies, until the Franchisee is again able to satisfy the Franchisor or the supplier that it is able to meet its payment obligations in the normal course of business. The Franchisee acknowledges that such steps in respect of suppliers may be required in order to preserve the buying relationship with that supplier for the benefit of the Franchisor and its other Franchisees.

Here, the Franchisor can require all supplies be distributed to you on a COD basis. This may be because the franchisor, through one of its subsidiary companies, is also the supplier of the product or service in question. Or it simply wishes to maintain good relations with the suppliers.

3.7 Substandard Supplies

In order to maintain quality, standardization, uniformity, and consistency among all EMMA & JEREMY'S Internet Café & Donut Emporiums, the Franchisor reserves the right, to require the Franchisee to remove from use at the Franchised Location any menu, food, or other items or supplies or products that do not conform to the Franchisor's specifications and quality control standards immediately upon written notice to that effect.

The franchisor can require that you remove substandard or unauthorized products for sale. This is a normal provision.

Some franchisors may allow you to purchase supplies from an alternative supplier as long as such product meets the franchisor's standards and specifications (i.e., it is not inferior) and for a finite period of time until the franchisor's own product becomes either more readily available or more competitively priced.

3.8 Suggested Prices

The Franchisor may from time to time suggest standard prices for products sold and services performed at the Franchised Location by the Franchisee. Except as hereafter provided, the Franchisee shall have the sole right to determine such prices and the Franchisee shall not suffer in the Franchisee's business relationship with the Franchisor or any other person over whom the Franchisor may have control if such price suggestions are not followed. Notwithstanding any other provision of this section 3.8, the Franchisee shall not at any time offer any products or services for sale at a price or rate in excess of the price or rate suggested by the Franchisor for such product or service at such time.

The *Competition Act* of Canada (a statute that has criminal law penalties) makes it an offence to restrict a franchisee or other seller as to how low a price they can sell a product for; such a restriction would serve to keep prices high and restrict competition. The language here reflects the law in that as a franchisee, you can sell for the lowest price you want, and you will not suffer in your business relationship with the franchisor for this.

8

FEES AND REPORTING

4. FEES AND REPORTING

4.1 Initial Franchisee Fee

As part of the consideration for the franchise rights granted hereunder, the Franchisee shall pay to the Franchisor an initial franchise fee (hereinafter called the "Initial Franchisee Fee") in the amount specified in Schedule "A" hereto, of which any deposit previously paid by the Franchisee shall form a part, and which shall be paid in full concurrently with the execution of this Agreement. The Initial Franchise Fee shall be deemed to have been fully earned by the Franchisor upon the granting of this franchise, and no portion of the Initial Franchise Fee shall be refundable to the Franchisee, except as otherwise specifically set forth herein.

The initial franchise fee is what the franchisor charges for the right to become a McDonald's, White Spot, Tim Hortons, or any other franchise. It is the price you pay to acquire the licence to use the franchisor's trade-mark, concept, and system for the initial term of the franchise. (Note that a franchise is not a tangible asset that banks lend money on and few, if any, financial institutions will take security or be able to take security in something as intangible as a licence.)

The range for initial franchise fee varies across the country depending upon the franchise in question, but in 2009, $18,500 to $25,000 seemed to be the going rate charged by small or start-up systems. More established and sought after franchise systems charge anywhere from $30,000 to $75,000. Don't forget, this is just the cost for the licensed rights to use the system and trade-marks for the initial term. Construction and development costs must be added to this number to get a sense of how much it costs to "open the doors."

Franchisors tend not to negotiate the initial franchise fee. It's really not in the franchisor's interest to lower the fee here and there. This is partially because franchisees in the system will compare deals, and if one franchisee obtained his or her rights for an initial fee of $20,000 and yet another franchisee paid $30,000 around the same time, this will create conflict in the system. (The franchisor will get some heated telephone calls.)

On limited occasions there may be some room to negotiate a reduction of the initial franchise fee in circumstances in which the franchisor is a start-up entity with few or no units in operation. It should be noted that the market for qualified franchisees is not large. There are not a large number of persons with business acumen, borrowing power, and $45,000 cash for the franchisor's initial franchise fee walking the streets of Canadian cities. Accordingly, a start-up franchisor who has set a $45,000 initial franchise fee may find that if it does not lower the fee, that very qualified lead is simply going to find another franchisor who will.

If a start-up franchisor with no established track record, no franchisees, and an unregistered trade-mark is seeking an initial franchise fee of $50,000, I would advise a potential franchisee that this is much higher than the current "going rate" and may be unjustifiable in the circumstances. You or your franchise lawyer can attempt to sway the franchisor and its lawyer in these circumstances.*

In a recent matter that I was involved with, a start-up franchisor was charging, in my view, far too much for its initial franchise fee. It was way out of line for a start-up system with no franchisees and a problem trade-mark. Instead of reducing the initial franchise fee, the franchisor granted the franchisee a very large exclusive territory (a municipality) and the right to locate a second location in that territory without a second franchise fee. This was a win-win outcome for both parties, as my client did not want to walk away from the deal.

Another approach for second and subsequent locations is to argue (politely) that if the initial franchise fee is designed to compensate the franchisor for training, such training may not be necessary for second and subsequent units in which the franchisor's principal has been trained when the first unit was acquired (e.g., "Why should I pay the full initial fee for my second outlet if you don't have to train me for it?") Some franchisors deal on this point; others direct the franchisee to the nearest lake and request that they jump!

4.2 Continuing Royalties

(a) In addition to the Initial Franchise Fee, and any other fee charged by the Franchisor, the Franchisee shall pay to the Franchisor a non-refundable monthly continuing royalty based upon a percentage of the Franchisee's gross sales from all products and services sold, rented, or dispensed at or from the Franchised Location (such payment is hereinafter called the "Continuing Royalties") in the manner

---

*Note: The figures represent my experience in 2009; these figures may increase by the time you read this book.

provided herein. The amount of Continuing Royalties to be paid by the Franchisee shall be the sum of 6 percent of the Franchisee's gross sales per month;

Franchise agreements will almost always contain some form of royalty, which is a monetary amount payable to the franchisor by you every week or every month, depending on the agreement. In support of royalties, one would have to say that the regular royalty keeps the franchisor financially able to administer the franchise system. Without the payment of the ongoing royalty, would the franchisor be financially viable? The franchisor has to make money as well, so royalties are justified. If you are using the franchisor's system and trade-mark, this comes at a price, and that price is the ongoing royalty.

No franchisee really likes paying a royalty, and franchisees like it even less if they are not receiving the support they expected from the franchisor. Whether the franchisee is receiving extensive support from the franchisor is largely irrelevant. From the franchisor's perspective, the royalty represents an ongoing payment by the franchisee for support provided by the franchisor, a payment for the use of the franchisor's system, and for the use of the franchisor's trade-mark. It is comparable to the payment of rent under a lease; the landlord may not be doing anything except collecting a cheque, but someone is using the property he or she owns. Here, the franchisee is using the property owned by the franchisor; its business systems and trade-mark.

Franchisors rarely, if ever, negotiate the amount of the royalty. This is because franchisees in the system will compare royalty rates, and if one franchisee is paying 5 percent and another is paying 6 percent, this will create conflict in the system.

(b)   For the purposes of this Agreement, "gross sales" shall mean the total revenues derived by the Franchisee in and from the Franchised Business, including cash sales and credit sales from the sale of products offered for sale and from the gross sales generated from any services performed at or from (whether directly or indirectly) the Franchised Location or the Franchised Business;

This definition has a problem and it's been deliberately done to illustrate a point. Royalties are almost always calculated as a percentage of the franchisee's gross sales for the monthly or weekly period. Accordingly, if gross sales at this location for the month of September were $50,000, the royalty of 6 percent due to the franchisor would be $3,000. But royalties are rarely if ever calculated on sales plus GST, PST, and legitimate returns. These amounts are normally subtracted from the total gross sales. So the definition of gross sales is normally amended to "carve out" refunds and returns and sales taxes such as GST, PST, and HST.

Be aware that some provinces restrict the amount of royalty that is calculated on liquor sales and paid to a franchisor (or other party). You may be prohibited by law paying the royalty specified in the franchise agreement on liquor sales. Check with the franchisor and your franchise lawyer, if you are using one.

Be cognizant of US or other foreign franchisors who provide that the currency of the agreement is in US dollars. All your gross sales will be in Canadian ones, and there will be exchange rate issues.

> (c) Payments of the Continuing Royalties shall be payable monthly on or before the tenth day of each month following the month in which such gross sales were made. All such payments shall be accompanied by a financial reporting statement showing how such Continuing Royalties were computed for the month in such form and detail and giving such other financial information as shall from time to time be required by the Franchisor;
>
> (d) The Franchisor may by written notice require the Franchisee to pay the Continuing Royalties for each monthly period by electronic transfer of funds or by pre-authorized payments from the bank account of the Franchisee to the bank account of the Franchisor. All electronic funds transfer or automatic pre-authorized bank payment plan costs shall be paid by the Franchisee. Any such notice may also require the Franchisee to make any or all other payments required to be made by the Franchisee to the Franchisor pursuant to this agreement by electronic funds transfer or automatic pre-authorized bank payment plan.

The franchisor may insist that royalties be payable by way of electronic funds transfer (EFT), which means, at week's end or month's end, the transfer of the appropriate royalty amount is instantaneously deducted from your bank account (usually when the franchisor is aware of the gross sales amount by means of a computerized "link-up" with your cash register). Payment by pre-authorized electronic bank transfer is standard. It avoids the necessity of having to send cheques in the mail.

Some franchisees believe that they can cancel the EFT because they don't agree with the franchisor's royalty amount or they are disputing the advertising fund. However, cancelling the EFT is a material breach under most agreements and could result in termination of the agreement. It is akin to withholding royalties.

If paid non-electronically, the normal provision would be for you to pay monthly royalties on the 10th or 15th day of the following month, together with the advertising fund contributions and other regular amounts that may be payable.

(e)   In the event that the Franchisee shall fail to report its monthly gross sales to the Franchisor as required for any month, the Franchisor shall have the right to estimate the amount of Franchisee's monthly gross sales for such period based upon the Franchisee's monthly gross sales for the preceding 2 months reported upon by the Franchisee (or for such lesser period as Franchisee shall have reported upon).

4.3   Quarterly Reporting

At the Franchisor's option, the Franchisee shall provide to the Franchisor on a quarterly basis, on or before the twentieth (20th) day of each month following each calendar quarter, an income and expense statement and a balance sheet in such form and detail as shall from time to time be reasonably required by the Franchisor in respect of the Franchised Business during the preceding calendar quarter.

The franchisor wishes to be in the position of not only assessing your performance from time to time and the categories of your sales (e.g., product X sells better at this location than product Y), but also to ensure that the royalty that it is receiving on gross sales is in fact accurate and not an amount pulled from the sky. Accordingly, there will be provisions within the franchise agreement obligating you to provide reports on gross sales for appropriate periods as well as profit and loss statements and balance sheets at specific points in time within the term (e.g., within 90 or 120 days after your fiscal year end). This is to be considered normal. Remote polling of sales by modem or other electronic means is also standard and should not be negotiated.

4.4   Annual Reporting

The Franchisee shall provide to the Franchisor on an annual basis, within ninety (90) days following the end of each fiscal year of the Franchisee, a balance sheet and a profit and loss statement for the Franchised Business for the preceding fiscal year, prepared in accordance with generally accepted accounting principles applied on a consistent basis from year to year, which shall be audited by a Certified Public Accountant.

Supplying financial statements each year to the franchisor is to be expected. The question is, what level of statement is reasonable? A full audit is a very expensive undertaking, and arguably unnecessary for what might well be a small owner-operated franchised business. Besides, if the franchisor believes you are misrepresenting your sales figures, it can audit your records itself pursuant to section 4.5, and if you have underreported by more than 3 percent, you have to pay for the audit and deal with the potential termination of your franchise. It is suggested here that either the requirement for audited financial statements be dropped from the franchise agreement in favour of unaudited, accountant certified financial statements, or some negotiate on take place that might require an audit only in exceptional circumstances (i.e., regular errors in gross sales calculation or other reasonable grounds).

A number of the franchise agreements that I have reviewed require the franchisee to provide to the franchisor on an annual basis audited financial statements prepared by a chartered accountant (CA). Many franchisees have pre-existing relationships with certified general accountants (CGA) and the franchise agreement shouldn't dictate the designation of your accountant if you use a CGA instead of a CA. In other words, you should be free to choose a certified general as opposed to a chartered accountant to prepare your financials.

You might be able to tell that section **4.4** above was taken from an agreement used in the United States where audit requirements are more prevalent and where they use the "certified pubic accountant" designation. (Accountants in Canada are normally designated as chartered accountants or certified general accountants. We don't have certified public accountants.) This brings up the point that many US legal concepts do not import well into a franchise agreement for use in Canada unless that agreement is adapted for use in Canada.

4.5   Verification and Audit Rights

The Franchisor shall have the right at any reasonable time to enter the Franchisee's business premises and to inspect, review, verify, and/or audit the business records of the Franchised Business. The Franchisee shall cooperate with the Franchisor and shall make all such business records available to the Franchisor including, but without limitation, electronic business records stored on disc, hard drive, CD-ROM, tape, or other medium. If the Franchisor shall review or audit the Franchisee's business records and if the Franchisee's gross sales as reported to the Franchisor should be found to be understated by more than three percent (3%), or if the Franchisee shall have failed to report its gross sales to the Franchisor as required, then the Franchisee shall pay to the Franchisor upon demand the cost of the review or audit as well as the additional amount payable as shown thereby.

There is normally a covenant whereby if the franchisor suspects that you have under-reported gross sales, the franchisor can direct that an audit occur of your business and if such error is greater than, for example, 3 percent, then the cost of that audit is passed on to you (and if the franchisor is wrong, it must pay). One or more instances of under-reporting may also bring about termination.

In any event, regular and accurate reporting requirements are an important obligation you will have in any franchised business. If you are of the view that "it's none of the franchisor's business," perhaps franchising is not in your best interest. Regular reporting goes with the territory. If you are deliberately under-reporting your gross sales, perhaps you deserve the strong medicine only an accountant's bill for an audit can deliver!

4.6 Overdue Payments

All overdue payments of the Franchisee shall bear interest from the due date until paid at the rate of eighteen percent (18%) per annum. All such overdue interest shall be calculated at the aforesaid effective annual rate and then paid to the Franchisor on a monthly basis.

Negotiating a lower interest rate for late payments only suggests that you will be a late payer. Leave this clause alone.

4.7 All Payments Net to the Franchisor

The Franchisee acknowledges that all monies required to be paid to the Franchisor under this Agreement (or any sublease, sign lease, equipment lease, or any computer system license) including, but without limitation, the Initial Franchise Fee and the Continuing Royalties, constitute the full amounts to be paid to the Franchisor, net of any goods and services taxes, provincial sales taxes, or other similar taxes that may be payable in connection therewith and which the Franchisee is liable to pay as required by applicable law in addition to the amounts required to be paid to the Franchisor.

This clause provides that all payments to the franchisor are net of tax and that you must add applicable GST and, depending on the province, PST, QST, or HST.

9

ADVERTISING

In addition to the payment of your continuing royalties, there is normally an obligation to pay some amount of your gross sales toward an "advertising fund." Royalties of 6 percent with an advertising fund contribution of 2 percent are not unusual although, for different industries and different systems, those numbers may vary.

The purpose of the advertising fund is to enable the franchisor to receive contributions from a number of franchisees within its system so that it can better afford expensive media advertising to the benefit of all franchisees and corporate stores in the system.

TV, radio, and large-scale newspaper advertising is where consumers meet the product and the brand. Media advertising is where the action is, and it's expensive. Elaborate newspaper or television advertisements showing a number of locations, or the franchisor's Internet website describing the entire franchise system may well be something that is paid for with an advertising fund.

The use of the Internet for advertising, and for selling goods and services for sale to the public, is an increasing medium in every aspect of business. Franchising is included in this. It is therefore important for you to know whether or not you can freely use the Internet for such purposes.

The Internet is just another vehicle used for advertising purposes and it should not come as any surprise to find that the franchise agreement gives the franchisor the right to control your uses of the Internet, just as the agreement controls or directs other forms of advertising undertaken by you.

In the same way that the franchise agreement provides for the franchisor to control where (i.e., territory) and how (i.e., business format) you conduct the franchised business, it is not unusual to find that the franchise agreement will also provide for the franchisor to be able to control where and how you conduct the franchised business over the Internet. The franchisor will have a say on how you can (or cannot) use the franchisor's trade-marks as part of an Internet domain name and on its website, and how you can conduct advertising over the Internet. In the same way that the franchisor desires consistency and uniformity in all of the traditional aspects of the franchised business operations, it should be expected that such controls will also be used by the franchisor to achieve the same degree of consistency and uniformity in your use of the Internet.

If the franchise agreement does not spell these items out, then you should seek clarification from the franchisor, and appropriate amendments to the franchise agreement, before assuming that the Internet can be freely used by you without the usual degree of controls and required approvals by the franchisor.

Respecting the advertising fund, it is important to ascertain whether the franchisor is administering the advertising fund itself and paying itself a management fee for such administration. You may want to find the answers to the following questions:

- How much of a management fee is being paid to the franchisor for managing the fund (if any)?

- What, specifically, does the franchisor spend the advertising fund monies on?

- Does the franchise agreement spell this out or is it referred to in the manuals?

- How is the money being held?

- Is it being held in a "segregated" bank account apart from the franchisor's regular account?

- Does the franchisor agree to provide regular accounting or financial statements to you detailing the receipts and expenditures of the advertising fund?

- Is there an "advertising council" comprised of franchisor and franchisee representatives whereby your input can be obtained as to how the advertising fund is spent?

- Are the franchisor's corporate stores contributing to the advertising fund to the same extent that the franchised outlets are? If not, why not? (A revealing point!)

- How and where is the money being spent? For example, a Toronto-based franchisor may well be vigorously advertising from the advertising fund in the *Toronto Star* and on Ontario television, but that may arguably not assist British Columbia-based franchisees where neither the *Toronto Star* nor Ontario television are normally or necessarily received.

• If there is a surplus in the advertising fund at the end of the year, is the franchisor obligated to carry it forward and spend it on advertising in the next year?

5. ADVERTISING

5.1 Advertising Compliance

The Franchisee recognizes the value and importance of advertising, public relations, promotion, and marketing in a uniform manner to the furtherance of business growth, stability, and the goodwill and public image of the Franchisee's Franchised Business and of all franchised businesses belonging to the EMMA & JEREMY'S System, and the Franchisee agrees to abide by any advertising provisions of this Agreement and within the Franchisor's Operations Manuals in furtherance thereof.

5.2 Opening Promotion/Store Opening Costs

The Franchisee shall expend an initial amount of $5,000 on a pre-opening and opening promotion campaign for the Franchised Location, to be carried out by the Franchisee immediately before and after the Franchised Location opens for business. The Franchisor will provide input and guidance to the Franchisee in the establishment and carrying out of the opening promotion.

Opening promotion is a good way to let customers know you are in business and that the location is open to the public. However, perhaps the franchisor could be persuaded to contribute funds towards your opening promotion as well.

5.3 Local Advertising Obligation

The Franchisee shall expend on a continuing monthly basis amounts for conducting its own ongoing local market advertising and promotion throughout the term of this Agreement equal to 2 percent of its monthly gross sales (hereinafter called the "Local Advertising Obligation"). The Franchisor may, at its reasonable discretion, require the Franchisee to provide quarterly reports to the Franchisor of its local advertising expenditures. Such reports shall be in such form and detail as shall from time to time be reasonably required by the Franchisor and shall be accompanied by reasonable proof of such expenditures having been made. If so required, the Franchisee shall forward such reports to the Franchisor on or before the tenth (10th) day of each month following each calendar quarter during the term of this Agreement.

There may also be a requirement for you to spend some amount of money toward local advertising in addition to your contributions to the advertising fund. This should be expected.

Ads in the local newspaper, flyers, and the like should satisfy this obligation. Fund advertising may improve brand awareness generally, but may not bring in local customers. Perhaps you should try to reach an agreement with the franchisor that some expenses count towards satisfying this obligation, for example, a local mall advertising fund contribution or Yellow Pages advertising.

5.4   Promotion Programs

The Franchisee agrees to cooperate and participate fully in all advertising and promotional programs reasonably designated by the Franchisor from time to time on an equal or proportionate basis with all other EMMA & JEREMY'S locations.

The advertising fund may also be used to develop new promotional products that are in turn purchased at cost by you (e.g., hats, pins, cups, T-shirts, and other products bearing the trade-mark). You would purchase the promotional products at cost and either sell or give away the products to your customers.

5.5   Franchisor's Advertising Methods and Materials

The Franchisor may from time to time acquire or develop and provide to the Franchisee advertising methods and materials, and may suggest methods of conducting the Franchisee's local market advertising and promotion. The Franchisor may offer some of such materials to the Franchisee, without obligation, for a reasonable standard charge. Where the Franchisee develops its own proposed advertising methods and materials, it shall submit same to the Franchisor at least two weeks prior to the date on which such advertising material is required by the Franchisee for the Franchisor's reasonable written approval prior to use. The Franchisor will not unreasonably or arbitrarily withhold or delay its approval to such advertising material.

The franchisor will likely have developed its own advertising templates, displays, and other merchandising materials that you can use in your own advertising. It's quite appropriate for the franchisor to supply this material at a cost. As the franchisor owns or controls the trade-marks, it has to be sure that any advertising you are undertaking for your local market is pursuant to the franchisor's standards for such trade-mark usage (i.e., use of the correct logo and colours, the advertising material is in good taste, etc.). Incorrect usage of the logo or trade-marks in your own local advertising (using the logo not as directed) may well be a default under the agreement.

You may want to design your own specific ad copy. In this clause, the franchisor must approve it two weeks before the franchisee requires it. Two weeks may seem to be a reasonable time for the franchisor to approve of your advertising, but the franchisor may have other priorities and not get around to it as fast as it could. Perhaps an amendment could be included to the effect that if the franchisor has not consented to the material within the stated two-week period, the franchisor is deemed to have approved it. This may persuade the franchisor to look at the material promptly, rather than the franchisor letting it sit on a desk and taking its time to give you an answer.

Note that when I say "amendment" to the franchise agreement, it needn't be a complicated amendment to the formal agreement. It could be something like a letter confirming that the franchisor agrees to something (and that this constitutes a modification to the contract).

5.6   Regional Co-operative Advertising

The Franchisor may from time to time develop or assist in the development of regional co-operative advertising, promotional, marketing, or public relations campaigns designed to promote and enhance the value of all EMMA & JEREMY'S locations operating in a region. The costs of such regional co-operative campaigns shall be in addition to the other expenditures set out herein, and the Franchisee agrees to promptly pay its proportionate share of such costs, based upon the number of participating EMMA & JEREMY'S locations. If fifty percent (50 %) of the EMMA & JEREMY'S locations in the region elect to participate in any such campaign, the Franchisee shall participate therein on an equal or proportionate basis, notwithstanding that the Franchisee may have indicated its desire not to participate during the campaign approval process.

5.7   Yellow Pages Advertising

In addition to the other advertising expenditures set out herein, the Franchisee shall at its own expense place and maintain throughout the term of this Agreement an advertisement in the local Yellow Pages directory best servicing the Franchised Location. Where there are other EMMA & JEREMY'S locations serviced by the same Yellow Pages directory, the Franchisee shall participate in such Yellow Pages advertising on an equal basis with all such other EMMA & JEREMY'S locations. Such Yellow Pages advertising shall conform to the Franchisor's advertising guidelines and shall contain such copy and be of such size as is reasonably designated or approved by the Franchisor from time to time. The Franchisor reserves the right to place the Yellow Pages advertising and to bill the Franchisee for its share of the costs of same where there are more than one EMMA & JEREMY'S locations to be listed in the same Yellow Pages directory. The Franchisor's invoices for such costs shall be paid by the Franchisee within seven (7) days.

Co-operative advertising in the Yellow Pages allows an entire regional group of franchisees (e.g., all franchisees that are located within the boundaries of the Calgary Yellow Pages) to advertise the franchise and their specific locations at the same time, and economically as well, as the cost for such advertising can be divided among the franchisees. This also assists the customer. If the customer is in North West Calgary, he or she isn't likely to patronize a franchised outlet in the South East. Co-operative advertising in the Yellow Pages promotes the brand and allows customers to find the location nearest to them. Will the franchisor also be contributing to Yellow Pages costs relating to its stores as well and to the same extent as the franchisees? But ask yourself this: Are the Yellow Pages even relevant in the age of Google?

5.8   Advertising Fund

(a)   The Franchisee shall contribute to a national advertising fund administered by the Franchisor (the "Advertising Fund") by paying to the Franchisor monthly, by the tenth (10th) day of each month following the month in which such gross sales were made, an amount equal to TWO PERCENT (2 %) of all gross sales made at or from the Franchised Location during the preceding month.

(b)   The Advertising Fund shall be administered and allocated by the Franchisor in its discretion and spent or reserved for expenditure exclusively on any and all aspects of advertising, marketing, promotion, and public relations relating to the EMMA & JEREMY'S System in such media and geographic areas, regionally, nationally, and/or internationally, as the Franchisor shall determine in its discretion from time to time.

(c)   The Franchisee's contributions to the advertising fund are non-refundable, and all such required contributions that remain unpaid from time to time shall remain payable and shall be paid by the Franchisee to the Franchisor even in the event that this Agreement shall expire or terminate for whatever reason.

(d)   Contributions to the advertising fund are in addition to all other payments required to be made by the Franchisee to the Franchisor hereunder, and failure to contribute to such fund by the Franchisee as and when required shall be deemed a material default hereunder.

(e)   Contributions to the advertising fund are subject to applicable federal Goods and Services Tax.

5.9   Administration of Costs and Accounting by the Franchisor

When instigated, the Franchisor shall administer and coordinate the use of the Advertising Fund and shall be entitled to charge a reasonable amount to the Advertising Fund, not to exceed fifteen percent (15%) of the total contributions to the fund, to cover its actual administrative and accounting expenses and overhead incurred in connection therewith. In the event that the Franchisor shall loan money to the Advertising Fund to cover advertising expenses, which are in excess of the amount of contributions received by the Franchisor for the Advertising Fund to date, the Franchisor shall be entitled to be repaid for any such loaned funds out of subsequent contributions made to the Advertising Fund. The Franchisor shall account for the Advertising Fund separately from its other funds, and shall maintain the Advertising Fund in a separate bank account segregated from its other funds. The Franchisor shall provide to the Franchisee a yearly accounting of the receipts and expenditures of the Advertising Fund, certified by an Officer of the Franchisor, within ninety (90) days following the Franchisor's fiscal year end. The Franchisor undertakes in administering the Advertising Fund to use its reasonable efforts to use the Advertising Fund for the benefit of all members of the EMMA & JEREMY'S System, however the Franchisee acknowledges that the Franchisor is under no obligation to use the advertising fund for the benefit of all contributors on an equal or proportionate basis to the amount contributed.

It is quite standard for the franchisor to establish an advertising fund to which all franchisees contribute money on a regular basis. The fund is based upon each franchisee's gross sales; the norm being anywhere from 1 to 4 percent of the franchisee's gross sales. It can be a flat fee as well. The franchisor in this example can charge the fund something for its own administration, which also is reasonably standard. In this case, the franchisor can charge the fund 15 percent.

The franchisor often supports the fund in the early days of the franchise; it loans the fund money to get the fund up to a level at which meaningful media advertising programs can be undertaken. Naturally, the franchisor is contractually entitled to a return of these loans at some point in time.

The management of the advertising fund is one of the top grievances franchisees have with their franchisors. It is important that the agreement contain a provision requiring a yearly accounting of the fund to be undertaken and the statements provided to you and the other franchisees in order that you can see where the advertising dollars have actually been spent and in what media. In this clause, the franchisor states that it will attempt to use the fund to the benefit of all franchisees in the system but cannot spend the fund on a pro rata or proportionate basis.

It's worth discussing the issue of the fund with the franchisor if you suspect your franchisor is going to spend the fund disproportionately and not in your region. Perhaps until the franchisor gets established in your province, the franchisor will agree to a greater percentage of your gross sales being spent on local advertising and less of a contribution towards the fund (a re-balancing). Or perhaps there is no requirement to contribute until the franchisor has established a sufficient number of units in your province.

10

INTELLECTUAL PROPERTY: TRADE-MARKS, TRADE SECRETS, AND COPYRIGHT

In addition to the franchisor's know-how, systems, and format, and the joint purchasing power available to members of a large system, the franchisor should also be licensing you the use of its trade-marks and other intellectual property rights.

Trade-marks are words, designs, or marks that distinguish one trader's wares or services in the marketplace from another's. Trade-marks are recognizable in every commercial setting and the billions of dollars spent each year in advertising are designed primarily to advertise trade-marks with the public so that an association is made between the trade-mark, the product, and the company, and value is built in the trade-mark and its associated goodwill. "The Keg" is a trade-mark, and so are White Spot, McDonald's, Tim Hortons, and Blenz. (Even, dare I say, "Martha Stewart" is a trade-mark.)

Not only is "Coca-Cola" a registered trade-mark both in words and script, but also the recognizable Coke bottle is a "distinguishing guise" and a trade-mark in and of itself. Numbers can be a trade-mark (e.g., "649" for lotteries); letters can be a trade-mark (e.g., "IBM" for computers); mere designs can be a trade-mark (e.g., the apple design used for the Macintosh computer); and slogans can be a trade-mark (e.g., "We do it all for you," "You're in the Pepsi generation," "Think Different," etc.).

From your perspective, it may be useful to ask particulars as to trade-mark registration and status (i.e., registration number and ownership). If the franchisor does not have a copy of the certificate of registration, you may be able to go online and check the status of the franchisor's trade-marks on the Strategis website maintained by the government of Canada. You should inquire whether there are any outstanding opposition or infringement actions that might affect the franchisor and you, although some of this may be ascertainable from the Strategis web search.

6. INTELLECTUAL PROPERTY

6.1 Licensed Rights

The franchise granted hereby is a license only, upon the terms and conditions contained herein, to use and display the EMMA & JEREMY'S System and the Trade-marks and trade name, and to use the Franchisor's copyright materials, Operations Manual, method of operation, format, and goodwill (the "Licensed Rights"), but only in connection with the Franchised Business operated by the Franchisee and only in accordance with the terms and conditions of this Agreement and any operational standards set by the Franchisor from time to time during the term of this Agreement (the "Standards"). Upon expiration or termination of this Agreement for any reason, the Franchisee shall surrender and deliver to the Franchisor all of the Licensed Rights, including physical possession of all objects bearing or containing the Trade-marks (or any word or design comprising the Trade-marks), and the Franchisee shall not thereafter use any of the Licensed Rights.

Section 6.1 reiterates in legal language the nature of the relationship. The franchisor is licensing the use of its system and trade-marks to you for the length of the term pursuant to the terms of the agreement, its confidential operations manual, and any standards established by the franchisor.

At the end of the term, you no longer have any rights to use the system and trade-marks, and they revert back to the franchisor unless the agreement is renewed or a new one is entered. This is the essential fact about franchising: you never buy your franchise. You can never own your franchise rights. You may own the tables and chairs and the refrigeration equipment, the ovens, and other business assets, but you simply have the licenced rights to use the franchisor's system and trademarks at the location for a period of years, paying the franchisor for those rights by way of the initial franchise fee and regular royalties. It's a little (but only a little) like a lease; the lease allows a tenant to use space as long as the tenant complies with the lease and pays rent.

6.2 Use of Trade-mark

(a) The Franchisee shall operate the Franchised Business under the name "EMMA & JEREMY'S" or as directed by the Franchisor from time to time. The Franchisee's own corporate name shall be clearly indicated on the Franchisee's advertising materials, business stationery, and other forms in a manner specified or reasonably approved by the Franchisor or as contained in the Operations Manual from time to time, and which clearly indicates that the Franchisee is the independent owner and operator of that business;

(b) The Franchisee shall use the Trade-marks only in their exact form and as prescribed in the Operations Manual from time to time, and the Franchisee shall indicate to the public in the manner directed by the Franchisor from time to time that the Trade-marks are owned by EMMA & JEREMY'S RESTAURANT LTD. and used by the Franchisee under license;

(c)   The Franchisee shall not use the words "Emma," "Jeremy," "E & J's" "Donut," or "Emporium," or any derivative thereof or any confusingly similar or colourably imitative words as part of the corporate or firm name of any corporation or other entity operating the Franchised Business pursuant to this Agreement, or any business operated by the Franchisee after the expiration or termination of this Agreement, nor will the Franchisee use the words "Emma," "Jeremy," "E & J's," "Donut," or "Emporium" as part of any web page or email address without the Franchisor's prior written consent; and

(d)   The Franchisee may only use the name EMMA & JEREMY'S in association with the Franchised Business, and all goodwill accruing to the use of the EMMA & JEREMY'S name and Trade-marks shall accrue to EMMA & JEREMY'S RESTAURANT LTD. as the owner and licensor thereof respectively.

Billions upon billions of dollars are spent each year on advertising. What is being advertised is the "brand" of a product or company in order that consumers recognize that brand and buy the products or services represented by it. Accordingly, it is very important for franchisors to ensure that their franchisees are using the franchisor's trade-marks as required by the franchisor and as required by law. Ensuring the marks or the distinctive elements of the marks (in this case the Emma/Jeremy's/Donut/Emporium combination) are not incorporated into the franchisee's corporate name and aren't used by the franchisee after the term has ended. The franchisor's trade-mark is a very valuable asset, and contractual requirements to protect that asset are both standard and desirable.

In other words, there is nothing to negotiate here, but note in this example, the owner of the trade-mark is not the franchisor, suggesting that the franchisor may be a master franchisee (acquiring its rights from another party), or the franchisor has a subsidiary company that owns the mark. It is certainly worth doing some due diligence on the ownership of the mark.

6.3   Other Trade-marks

For the purposes of this Agreement, references to the Trade-marks shall include any additional, substitute, or modified trade-marks hereafter adopted by the Franchisor and authorized, designated, and licensed for use by the Franchisee in connection with the Franchised Business. If at any time during the term of this Agreement the Franchisor shall deem it advisable to modify or discontinue use of any trade-mark, or to adopt and use any additional or substitute trade-marks, then it shall give notice in writing to the Franchisee to that effect, and the Franchisee shall be obligated to comply with all such reasonable changes at the Franchisee's own expense and within such time as is reasonably allowed by the Franchisor in the circumstances.

The franchisor may change the trade-mark or may choose another trade-mark if it believes the system requires a new mark. Sometimes franchised systems, like people, must re-invent themselves, and having the right to change the mark is of importance to the franchisor. But remember that brand re-identification or the adoption of a new mark will involve money. Signs must be changed and advertising material must be altered. You will be required to pay for your own signage change costs.

6.4   Operations Manual

The Franchisor shall furnish the Franchisee on loan with its current Operations Manual and all other related manuals then in current use upon the execution of this Agreement or as soon thereafter as is reasonably practicable. All such manuals may be revised from time to time. The Franchisee agrees to maintain all such manuals, as revised, at the premises from which it operates the Franchised Business, and to only give access thereto to its employees directly involved in operating the Franchised Business. The Franchisee shall surrender and deliver possession of all such manuals to the Franchisor upon expiration or termination of this Agreement. The Operations Manual as revised from time to time and any other manual developed by the Franchisor as part of the System is hereby incorporated into this Agreement by reference. In the event of a discrepancy, the manuals as maintained by the Franchisor with all current revisions shall be the governing copies.

The franchise agreement is an important document governing the relationship between the franchisor and you but it is not the only document. The franchise agreement cannot explain how long to cook the French fries, how to operate the computer system, when to flip the steaks, portion control on the pizza, inventory control issues, ordering forms, style and colour of advertising material, financial reporting forms and the like. These matters are normally included in the franchisor's operations manual.

Established franchise systems will always have sophisticated and comprehensive operations manuals, whether in print form, on CD-ROM, or by way of a secure dedicated web access. Start-up franchisors may not have developed their manual systems, and some might not even see the need for one.

If there is a system, that system should have a manual — if for any other reason, so that the day-to-day operation of the system can be taught (i.e., how long to cook the pizza, portion control, etc.) to you and your employees.

Ask other franchisees in the system how helpful or comprehensive the manuals are. Try and see if the franchisor will show you the manuals in advance, although it may be reluctant owing to confidentiality.

6.5   Confidential Information

The Franchisee acknowledges that the materials, information, specifications, the Standards forming part of the EMMA & JEREMY'S System, including the Franchisor's Operations Manual, the specifications, and standards for products, inventory, supplies, equipment, and list of designated or approved suppliers, forms and internal communications are protected by copyright, are proprietary to the Franchisor and confidential and constitute trade secrets that the Franchisee shall not use for any purpose inconsistent with this Agreement or publish or reveal to any unauthorized party during the term of this Agreement or thereafter for such period of time as such matters remain confidential and not in the public domain. The Franchisor reserves the right at any time upon written notice to the Franchisee to more particularly specify or define any elements or items of information or materials that the Franchisor considers to be confidential trade secrets for the purposes of the ongoing application and survival of the Franchisee's covenants herein. The covenants of this paragraph shall also extend to cover and bind each director, officer, and principal of the Franchisee who has in any capacity affixed his or her signature to this Agreement.

You may have executed a covenant of confidentiality in a deposit agreement. The franchise agreement will contain a far more comprehensive provision. The franchisor seeks to ensure that its business system does not fall into the hands of a competitor, especially if that competitor is a current or former franchisee. This very legitimate provision is your legal agreement to keep all aspects of the franchise confidential, including manuals, know how, etc.

There is nothing to negotiate here, but note that the clause above seems to suggest the directors, officers, and principals of the franchisee who have signed the agreement (on behalf of a corporate franchisee) are personally bound to these covenants of confidentiality. In fact, if a franchisor requires a covenant of confidentiality from an individual, that individual has to sign the agreement in his or her individual capacity. Nevertheless, I wouldn't argue with the above provision. To negotiate matters dealing with intellectual property might suggest that you're interested in the intellectual property more than you're interested in the franchise rights.

It is in the best interests of the system that matters pertaining to the system be held in confidence. However, in a clause such as this, the franchisor may claim that all sorts of information is confidential, but not everything claimed to be confidential is legally confidential information. For instance, what you know from your past employment or business is not confidential to the current franchisor; matters or procedures generally known in the industry are not confidential. You cannot unlearn what you have learned.

6.6 Environmental and Health Standards Respecting Food Handling and Disposal

The Franchisee and the Guarantor shall be fully responsible for compliance with all applicable health and environmental laws, regulations, ordinances, permit requirements, and policies under applicable federal, provincial, and municipal laws, and under any lease or sublease, respecting the storage, preparation, handling and disposal of food products, and other products. The Franchisee and the Guarantor hereby jointly and severally indemnify and hold the Franchisor harmless from and against all claims, demands, and liabilities of whatever nature and kind arising out of any non-compliance by the Franchisee of such health and environmental laws, regulations, ordinances, permit requirements, policies, and lease provisions.

Certain businesses require compliance with specific laws. For example, the restaurant business normally requires compliance with laws pertaining to health, safety, food handling, and liquor licensing.

Other sorts of franchised businesses might require a franchisee to specifically comply with waste management and environmental protection laws (e.g., a muffler shop or lube business). Because environmental statutes impose liability to a wide assortment of persons and entities, the franchisor here is obtaining an indemnity from both the franchisee and the guarantor for any failure to comply with such regulations.

11

THE OBLIGATIONS OF THE FRANCHISOR AND FRANCHISEE

7. TRAINING

7.1 Training of the Franchisee

(a) The Franchisor shall furnish training to two persons who are owners, managers, or employees of the Franchised Business with sufficient initial training in respect of the management and operation of a EMMA & JEREMY'S Franchised Business and the methods and techniques of the System. The Franchisor's training program and on-site location assistance comprises of approximately one week's training in the EMMA & JEREMY'S System, and in particular, training of such designated persons in the following areas:

   (i) Food service, EMMA & JEREMY'S recipes, food handling, and preparation;

   (ii) Customer service;

   (iii) Store management procedures; and,

   (iv) Use of computer system.

The training provision is not something you would normally seek to negotiate with your franchisor. You only know if training is sufficient to operate the franchised business successfully after you have attended and completed the training and tried to operate the business.

Often established franchise companies will have extremely comprehensive training programs, lasting between one and several months. I am encouraged by long training programs as it suggests that the franchisor in question is serious about ensuring the franchisee will be able to successfully operate the franchisor's business system. They have an investment in their franchisees, and want them to succeed. A comprehensive training program goes a long way to ensure that the franchisee will be successful.

When the agreement specifies a training period of only three days, for example, you must question how you can be trained to do anything in that short period of time. This is where it is important to discuss this matter with existing franchisees of the system. Ask them if the training was comprehensive enough to enable them to commence operation of the business.

Assess from the franchisor how many people can be trained. The franchisor has to pay for the franchisee to be trained (i.e., it has to dedicate resources, a physical facility, and training personnel), but the franchisor can't be expected to train seven representatives of the franchisee. It's usually one or two representatives of the franchisee, such as a husband and wife, or owner and manager.

If it seems prudent to have another member of your business organization trained, assess that cost with the franchisor. The training provided by the franchisor should also be "training the trainer training." That is to say, the franchisor should train you so that you can train your own employees.

> (b)   The training shall be given at a location designated by the Franchisor, who shall give the Franchisee at least one (1) weeks' notice of the date and place of such training. The Franchisor will pay no compensation for any services performed by trainees during such training and all expenses incurred by the Franchisee or the trainees in connection with such training shall be for the account of the Franchisee. Such persons must also make their own travel and accommodation arrangements, as travel and accommodation costs are not provided by the Franchisor;

Note that there is no salary or other compensation payable to you during the training period. Note also that the training will be at a facility available to the franchisor, which might be in a different province from where you live and intend to establish the franchised business. In other words, if you are living in Abbotsford, British Columbia, and establishing your business in that area, you may find that you have to travel and stay in Toronto for four weeks to attend and complete the training. You will have to make your own living arrangements in Toronto for that period of time and you will not be paid while you are trained there.

> (c)   The Franchisee and its staff members (which shall include the owner-operators specified in Schedule "A") shall satisfactorily complete such training prior to the commencement of the Franchised Business. The Franchisee acknowledges that the Franchisor's training programs and materials are proprietary confidential information forming part of the EMMA & JEREMY'S System;

In some franchise agreements there will be a provision where if the franchisor determines that you are not capable of being trained, then the franchisor may terminate the franchise agreement and return all or a significant portion of your initial franchise fee. In this instance, the franchisor has reserved the right to determine whether or not you are an acceptable franchisee through the training process, and if you are not, then the franchisor can terminate the agreement based on your performance at the training session. This is not unusual, although it's extremely complicated if you have already leased premises and built out the location. It is not ridiculous to question what might happen if you don't complete the training successfully. Certainly, it is not in the franchisor's interest to have a poorly performing or a poorly trained franchisee.

(d)   If additional assistance or training over and above that normally furnished by the Franchisor is required or requested by the Franchisee at any time, the Franchisor and the Franchisee shall discuss and reasonably agree upon what is required and the Franchisor will furnish such additional assistance or training. The Franchisor reserves the right to charge a reasonable standard fee, together with its reasonable expenses incurred in providing such additional assistance or training; and

In some circumstances, if you require additional training, the franchisor will provide it, but only at a cost. There will also be provisions within the franchise agreement, like the provisions noted above, that indicate that the franchisor will provide "on-going assistance" from time to time. Unless it is clear in the franchise agreement, it should be established what sort of on-going assistance will be given. It should also be understood what triggers a "fee" and what does not, as often the on-going assistance provision entitles the franchisor to charge a fee for its services, plus expenses.

(e)   The Franchisee may require additional training in circumstances where this agreement is renewed and may also deem that no training is required in such circumstances or in circumstances where the Franchisee is an EMMA & JEREMY'S Operator at a different location. In any event, no reduction to the Initial Franchise Fee shall be made where no training is provided.

Lastly, some franchise agreements separate the initial franchisee fee from a "training fee." That is, the initial franchise fee may be $30,000 but the training fee is an additional $10,000. Part of the reason for this is because franchisees in a system might take over more than one location but don't believe that they need to be trained for the second and third locations. If the initial franchisee fee is meant to compensate the franchisor in part for its training, then segregating out the initial franchise fee from the training fee allows multiple unit franchisees to save this cost.

8.   FRANCHISOR'S GENERAL OBLIGATIONS

8.1   General Obligations

(a)   The Franchisor shall furnish the Franchisee with:

   (i)   one (1) copyrighted Operations Manual on loan for use in the Franchised Business and all revisions thereof made by the Franchisor from time to time;

Successful franchises are often those in which the concept can be put into a manual and easily taught to the franchisee. Accordingly, franchising may be successful in restaurant, fast-food, hotel, income tax preparation, camera stores, and other industries but unsuccessful in industries in which the business is simply too complicated or cannot be reduced to writing in the form of a manual.

Although the franchisor's operations manual is normally confidential property constituting a trade secret owned by the franchisor, it should be established that the franchisor, especially in a start-up system, actually has an operations manual that will be delivered to you on loan (or accessible by Internet or CD-ROM) once the franchise agreement has been signed.

   (ii)   advertising, marketing, and promotional methods and materials acquired or developed by the Franchisor from time to time, and the Franchisor's suggested methods of conducting the Franchisee's local market advertising and promotion;

   (iii)   periodic communications regarding new ideas and developments pertinent to the Franchised Business; and

   (iv)   periodic visits to the Franchised Location for the purposes of consultation, assistance, and guidance of the Franchisee. The Franchisor's representatives will prepare written reports in respect of such visits for the benefit of both the Franchisor and the Franchisee outlining any suggested changes or improvements in the operation of the Franchised Business and detailing any defaults in such operations that become evident as a result of any such visit, and a copy of each such written report shall be provided to both the Franchisor and the Franchisee.

(b)   The Franchisor shall furnish the Franchisee with its specifications and quality standards in respect of products, services, supplies, inventory, suppliers, and equipment, including its list of designated or approved suppliers, which may be amended from time to time; and

(c) The Franchisor shall continue to be available at its office for consultation and guidance of the Franchisee at no charge in respect of the operation and management of the Franchised Business.

(d) The Franchisor will, from time to time, conduct market research and testing to determine consumer trends and the performance, quality, and marketability of new products and services. The Franchisee agrees to co-operate by participating in such market research and by using or test marketing new products and services at the Franchised Location from time to time and providing the Franchisor with information as requested. In connection with any such test marketing, the Franchisee agrees to purchase a reasonable quantity of the test products and to use or effectively display and make a reasonable effort to sell such products. At the end of the test marketing period, the Franchisee shall have the right to return unused, undamaged, and unsold non-perishable products still in good and saleable or usable condition to Franchisor within thirty (30) days for full credit equal to Franchisee's invoiced cost thereof.

You will note that the obligations undertaken by the franchisor in Article 8 are not particularly extensive. Franchise agreements are, after all, written by the franchisor's lawyers. It is in the franchisor's interest to agree to as little as possible, so you will see here that it's obligated to provide the manual, to provide advertising material, to communicate from time to time regarding new ideas, to periodically visit the franchised location and make suggestions, to provide quality standards, and that it will be available at its office for consultation. From its perspective, the franchisor is supplying the "business system" and the trade-marks for the franchisee to use.

Your obligations as the franchisee prescribed in the following section **9.1** are far more extensive and comprehensive than the obligations of the franchisor in section **8.1**. All of the provisions contained in section **9.1** are standard provisions you would find in virtually any Canadian franchise agreement. You must operate the business according to law and according to the franchisor's business system and standards. In many ways this is a repetition of other provisions within the agreement, but this section will contain more specific agreements by you such as paying your suppliers on time and dealing with them in an honest and ethical manner, making sure the premises is clean and all machinery is working, having adequately trained staff, maintaining an adequate supply of inventory, not using the premises for anything other than the franchised business, allowing the franchisor to inspect the premises, using uniforms as prescribed by the franchisor, and a host of other obligations.

9.   FRANCHISEE'S CONTINUING OBLIGATIONS

9.1   Obligations

In addition to any other obligations of the Franchisor prescribed hereunder:

(a)   The Franchisee shall operate the Franchised Business in compliance with all applicable laws, and in particular, all health, food handling, environmental, and work safety laws and regulations prescribed by federal, provincial, or local government agencies;

(b)   The Franchisee shall advertise and operate the Franchised Business and deal with all customers and suppliers in an honest and ethical manner;

(c)   The Franchisee shall comply with all specifications, standards, operating procedures, techniques, policies, and systems prescribed by the Franchisor from time to time in respect of the operation of the Franchised Business, and the Franchisee acknowledges and agrees that all such specifications, standards, operating procedures, techniques, policies and systems are the essence of the EMMA & JEREMY'S System, and that strict compliance by the Franchisee is important and valuable to the Franchisor and to all other Franchisees in order to maintain the uniformity and integrity of the EMMA & JEREMY'S System. Specifications, standards, operating procedures, techniques, policies, and systems prescribed from time to time by the Franchisor and set out in the Operations Manual, the Standards, or otherwise communicated to the Franchisee in writing shall constitute provisions of this Agreement as if they were fully set forth herein;

An example of a system prescribed by the franchisor might be that it requires you to instigate an electronic funds transfer system for automatic payment of royalties and other monies owing to the franchisor. If this is instigated in year three of a five-year term, it may come as somewhat of a surprise (and perhaps an expense) to you. Essentially, you are agreeing to conduct business according to the franchisor's system and method of doing business. If you are not prepared to conduct business pursuant to the franchisor's system and plan, perhaps you should be involved in another type of business, or in your own business and not a franchised business.

(d)   The Franchisee shall adopt and use the Franchisor's standard menu of products and services offered for sale at all EMMA & JEREMY'S Internet Café & Donut Emporium locations from time to time, and the Franchisee shall further adopt and use the Franchisor's standard format and design for the display of such menu and menu items at the Franchised Location, in accordance with the EMMA & JEREMY'S System together with all changes thereto from time to time designated by Franchisor by written notice to Franchisee to that effect;

(e)   The Franchisee shall maintain the condition and appearance of the Franchised Location premises and of all signs and equipment used in the Franchised Business, and the Franchisee shall carry out maintenance, repairs and replacements as required on a continuing basis, and shall make reasonable changes and improvements as the Franchisor may reasonably require during the term of this Agreement in order to maintain the condition and appearance and upgrade the Franchised Business to the Franchisor's then current image, standards, and specifications;

(f)   The Franchisee shall maintain at all times a sufficient number of adequately trained personnel to properly service all customers of the Franchised Business;

(g)   The Franchisee and its personnel shall perform all operations of the Franchised Business in a health conscious, safe, and responsible manner;

(h)   The Franchisee shall maintain an adequate supply of inventory, products, and other supplies sufficient to satisfy customer demand and to operate efficiently the Franchised Business;

(i)   The Franchisee shall keep the Franchised Location open for business during the normal business hours on all normal business days as reasonably prescribed by the Franchisor from time to time for the EMMA & JEREMY'S System, subject to compliance with applicable laws and the lease or sublease of the Franchised Location, (it being acknowledged and agreed that "normal business hours" for a EMMA & JEREMY'S Internet Café & Donut Emporium could entail Sunday opening and later night closings);

If you expect to be closed Sundays or close at 6:00 on weekdays, this should be canvassed by you, as the franchisor may have different expectations and the lease itself may require more extensive hours of operation.

(j)   The Franchisee shall continuously use the Franchised Location premises only as and for an EMMA & JEREMY'S Internet Café & Donut Emporium during the term of this Agreement;

(k)   The Franchisor shall have the right at any reasonable time to enter the Franchised Location and to inspect, review, and verify the operation of the Franchised Business in order to determine the Franchisee's compliance with this Agreement, and the Franchisee shall co-operate with the Franchisor for such purposes;

(l)   The Franchisee and those owner operators specified in Schedule "A" shall devote its and their full time and best efforts to actively conducting the Franchised Business at the Franchised Location in accordance with the terms and conditions of this Agreement;

If you don't intend to make this franchised business your full-time job, then the "full-time and best efforts" clause must be modified. The full-time best efforts clause might well prevent you from buying another business, notwithstanding the fact that your franchised business is running swimmingly.

> (m)   The Franchisee agrees to procure and maintain during the term of this Agreement insurance against the insurable risks and for not less than the amounts of coverage that may be specified by the Franchisor from time to time, and in particular, the Franchisee agrees to procure and maintain the following insurance coverage:

Often, the insurance requirements under a franchise agreement are long and extensive provisions lasting several pages. The franchisor is simply requiring you to maintain a sufficient amount of insurance to protect your business and also to protect the franchisor from its "royalty stream income" should fire or other casualty damage your business. These sorts of insurance provisions, however, may in fact cost you a considerable amount of money in premiums, which have increased since 9/11. It is suggested here that the insurance provisions be taken to your insurance agent and "priced out" so you are aware of what the insurance will cost. Many of these insurance clauses were drafted in the days before 9/11 and higher insurance premiums, and even the lawyers drafting these insurance clauses have no idea how much this coverage costs.

It is a good idea to always review the insurance clause with your insurance agent and assess both the coverage and the cost of the policy. It may well be that a clause applicable in an American contract is either inapplicable in Canada, or the premiums are so inordinately high that you will be unable to secure such coverage on an economic basis. You should also inquire as to whether or not the franchisor has or intends to have mandatory or optional group insurance coverage available to you.

> (i)   insurance coverage on a generally accepted "all risks" form for the Franchised Location premises and the leasehold improvements therein, and the equipment, fixtures, furnishings, software and hardware, signs, supplies, and inventory used in the Franchised Business to their full new replacement cost;
>
> (ii)   workers' compensation insurance as required by applicable law;
>
> (iii) comprehensive general liability insurance against civil public liability, including personal and bodily injuries or death and damage to or destruction of property in at least the amount of at least Two Million Dollars ($2,000,000) per person or occurrence with no aggregate coverage limits and with the following additional endorsements or coverage: personal injury liability; non-owned automobile; blanket contractual liability; contingent employer's

liability; products liability; completed operations liability; occurrence basis property damage; and employees added as additional insureds; and

(iv) tenant's legal liability insurance on a generally accepted all risks form in at least the amount specified in the lease for the Franchised Location premises.

(v) all such policies of insurance shall name the Franchisor as an additional insured, and shall apply as primary coverage and not as excess to any other insurance available to the Franchisor; and shall contain a waiver of the insurer's rights of subrogation in respect of any claim against the Franchisor; and (if reasonably available) shall not contain any exclusion clause for the claims of one insured versus another insured or for the acts of one insured affecting another insured, but instead shall contain a severability of interests clause and a cross liability clause whereby each such policy shall be treated as though a separate policy had been issued to each insured; and shall provide that the Franchisor shall receive at least thirty (30) days prior written notification of any cancellation, termination, expiry, amendment, or modification thereof that is material to this Agreement; and shall have deductible limits that do not exceed Two Thousand Dollars ($2,000) per person or event;

(vi) the Franchisee shall provide certificates evidencing such required insurance coverage to the Franchisor prior to commencing the Franchised Business and prior to each expiry date of such insurance policies;

(vii) the Franchisee may also obtain such other or additional insurance as it deems proper in connection with its operation of the Franchised Business;

(viii) nothing contained herein shall be construed as a representation or warranty by the Franchisor that such insurance as may be specified by the Franchisor from time to time will insure the Franchisee against all insurable risks or amounts of loss that may or can arise out of or in connection with the operation of the Franchised Business; and

(ix) maintenance of any such insurance and compliance by the Franchisee with its obligations under this paragraph shall not relieve the Franchisee of its liability under the indemnity provisions of this Agreement.

(n) The Franchisee shall compensate the Franchisor in an amount specified by the Franchisor (but not to exceed in total, $1,000 plus applicable taxes), for the preparation and documentation of this Franchise Agreement, and for the preparation and documentation of any Sublease and other agreement prepared by the Franchisor or the Franchisor's solicitors in respect of the grant and documentation of this franchise.

In many franchise agreements, the franchisor does not charge for the preparation of the franchise and other agreements. This falls within the initial franchise fee.

In other franchise agreements, the franchisor wishes to "offload" its legal expenses and pass on the expenses of creating a document package, which is prepared by the franchisor's lawyers. No doubt there is legal time in creating a document package for a new franchisee. Not only must this be drawn up by franchisor's counsel with accurate information concerning the identity of the franchisor, the guarantors, the precise length of the term, the location of the premises, and other matters, but the package must be executed by the franchisee and the guarantors, and the franchisor's lawyer must ensure that execution has been attended to and that there is an enforceable agreement once all the documents have been signed and returned.

More and more, Canadian franchise agreements are including a provision whereby the franchisee must pay all or some of these costs, which range from $1,500 to $2,500, in most cases. This may well be something that can be negotiated out of the franchise agreement; the argument being that the franchisor is being compensated by way of the initial franchise fee.

12

TRANSFER AND ASSIGNMENT
OF YOUR FRANCHISE

The transfer and assignment provisions are among the most lengthy and complicated parts of most franchise agreements. Virtually every franchise agreement contains an assignment clause, which places many restrictions upon your ability to sell the franchised business and transfer the franchise agreement to the buyer. This is very standard, but must be reviewed and understood by you from day one, because they will often become very important later on during the term of the agreement when you might wish to sell the business.

10. TRANSFER AND ASSIGNMENT

10.1 Assignment by the Franchisor

The Franchisor reserves the right to assign this Agreement in good faith to any party who, in the Franchisor's reasonable judgment, is financially and operationally capable of assuming the role of the Franchisor and performing the covenants and obligations to the Franchisee hereunder, and who agrees in writing to assume and be bound by and perform all of the terms, provisions, covenants, conditions, and obligations of this Agreement for the balance of the term and all renewal terms. The Franchisor shall give reasonable written notice of any such assignment to the Franchisee, whereupon the Franchisor shall have no further obligation or liability to the Franchisee under or in connection with this Agreement whatsoever.

Although you, as a franchisee, will always require the franchisor's consent for any sale or assignment of your franchise business, the franchisor requires no such consent and can sell its right in the franchised business to any entity it desires. This supports the position of many who claim that life's not fair.

10.2 Assignment by the Franchisee

The Franchisee acknowledges that this Agreement is a personal one, being entered into by the Franchisor in reliance upon and in consideration of the personal skills and qualifications of the Franchisee and the owner-operator(s) specified in Schedule "A," and the representations of same that have inspired the Franchisor's trust and confidence in the Franchisee and the Guarantor who will actively and substantially participate in the ownership and operation of the Franchised Business. Accordingly, this Franchise is not transferable or assignable in any manner, directly or indirectly, in whole or in part by the Franchisee without the prior written consent of the Franchisor. The Franchisor will not refuse to consent to a proposed assignment unless the Franchisee or the proposed assignee fail to meet the Franchisor's conditions of assignment as set out in Section 10.3 herein, and such consent will not be unreasonably withheld.

The provisions for assignment by you in the franchise agreement are more comprehensive and are similar to the provisions governing renewal. For instance, you will not be entitled to assign the agreement if you are in default under the franchise agreement or any other agreement between the parties. Your default constitutes grounds under which the franchisor need not consent to an assignment (or for that matter, a renewal). I think this is quite fair. If you are in default, why should the franchisor allow you to sell your business without you curing the default first?

It is in the interest of the franchisor that the new franchisee (called here the "assignee") is acceptable to the franchisor. The franchisor has no obligation to accept as an assignee someone who the franchisor would not ordinarily choose as a franchisee. Accordingly, the assignee will undergo the same evaluation that a new franchisee would undergo, and this is quite legitimate. Indeed, choosing the wrong franchisee is a recipe for disaster to the franchisor and the entire franchised system, so it's very important that the assignee (new franchisee) be evaluated by the franchisor to ensure that he or she has the financial and business background necessary to operate the franchised business and to fit in the system.

By the same token, however, the franchisor cannot use the assignment provision as an excuse to deny you the ability to sell your franchise. Both you and the franchisor must "act reasonably." There is case law respecting the issue of whether the franchisor has denied its consent to assign "unreasonably." These days, franchise agreements usually contain extensive criteria, which you and the assignee must meet in order for the franchisor to grant its consent to assignment. These conditions are noted in section **10.3**.

10.3 Conditions of Assignment

The Franchisor's consent to any assignment shall not constitute a waiver of any claim against the Franchisee or the Guarantor. The Franchisor's consent to any assignment shall be conditional upon the following:

(a)   The assignee shall reasonably meet the Franchisor's then current criteria for the selection and approval of Franchisees.

These criteria can change over time. It may be more difficult to qualify as a franchisee in the system now than it was five years ago. You should be aware of this.

(b)   The assignee, its owner-operator(s) and the management personnel proposed to be employed by the assignee for the Franchised Business shall satisfactorily complete the Franchisor's initial training program as set out herein (at the cost of the Franchisee).

There's no question that the assignee (who is becoming the new franchisee) should be trained by the franchisor in the operations and workings of the system in the same way that new franchisees are trained. It's normal for the franchisor to charge something for this training. Perhaps it will be reflected in the assignment fee paid to the franchisor, or perhaps there's a separate training fee that must be paid upon assignment. The question is, who pays for this training? Is it the existing franchisee selling the business or is the new franchisee buying the business?

(c)   The assignee shall assume and agree in writing to be bound by and perform all of the covenants and obligations of the Franchisee hereunder, or if required by the Franchisor, shall execute and deliver to the Franchisor a new form of Franchise Agreement for the remaining portion of the term of this Agreement. Such new Franchise Agreement may be in the Franchisor's then current standard form, which may include terms and conditions, which differ substantially from those contained in this Agreement.

The assignee may be asked to sign the franchisor's then-current standard form of franchise agreement. The assignee needs to be aware that the new agreement may contain higher rates for royalty or advertising fund payments and it may be in a different form than the agreement that the original franchisee signed some years earlier. Franchisors regularly modify and update their form of franchise agreements and the parties should be aware that the assignee may be required to go on the new form.

> (d) All obligations of the Franchisee under this Agreement and under any other agreement between the Franchisor and the Franchisee shall be brought up to date and into full compliance.

This essentially means that you must pay any and all monies that are due and owing up to the time of assignment, and perform such other obligations that you were required to perform up to the date of assignment. Otherwise the franchisor is not required to provide its consent. This is only fair. Why should the franchisor consent to the assignment of a franchise agreement if you are behind in royalty payments or are otherwise in default?

> (e) The Franchisee and the Guarantor shall deliver to the Franchisor a complete release of all claims against the Franchisor, EMMA & JEREMY'S INTERNET CAFÉ & DONUT EMPORIUM LTD. and its respective officers, directors, and affiliated corporations in respect of all matters arising under or pursuant to this Agreement.

As the existing franchisee, you are not "released" from your obligations under the franchise agreement by way of assignment. For example, Mr. A may sell to Mr. B, but if Mr. B defaults, then the franchisor has recourse against Mr. A and can sue Mr. A for the damages suffered by it.

It is extremely important to remember that unless you are released from your obligations, you are on the hook for any defaults committed by the new franchisee. If it's at all possible, you might try and obtain a full release of your obligations from the franchisor so the franchisor's only recourse is against the new franchisee. This may be difficult to obtain. Certainly your purchase agreement with the assignee should contemplate the possibility of a default and perhaps be dealt with by way of a personal indemnity by the principal of the assignee. Or perhaps even some form of holdback could be possible. But these are issues you would discuss with your purchaser.

Ideally, at the time of assignment, it is preferable for you to obtain a "full release" from the franchisor. This is not something that would be negotiated at the time you enter the franchise agreement, but at the time of assignment. Also you and the guarantor are required to release the franchisor from any liability as a condition to assignment. The franchisor does not want to consent to assignment only to be sued by a disgruntled former franchisee.

> (f) The Franchisee shall deliver to the assignee the Operations Manual, and all other materials of a confidential or proprietary nature relating to the EMMA & JEREMY'S System or bearing the Trade-marks.

(g)   The assignee shall not use in its corporate or firm name the words "Emma," "Jeremy," and/or any derivative thereof, or any words confusingly similar thereto or colourably imitative thereof.

(h)   The Franchisor reserves the right to require that the Franchisee or the assignee carry out such reasonable changes and improvements to the Franchised Location premises, equipment, and signs used in the Franchised Business as the Franchisor shall specify in order to upgrade the Franchised Business to the Franchisor's then current image, standards, and specifications.

The franchisor has the right to require the franchisee/assignee to upgrade the premises upon assignment to its then current image, standards, and specifications. This could cost money and is perhaps a provision that could be capped in advance. Renovations can be required by both the franchisor and the landlord, so if you are buying an existing franchised business from the franchisee (rather than from the franchisor), you probably need to establish whether renovation and refurbishment is likely to be required.

10.4   Assignment Fee

The Franchisee acknowledges that the Franchisor will incur expenses in connection with any assignment or proposed assignment, and thus the Franchisee shall reimburse the Franchisor for its reasonable actual expenses incurred in connection with the assignment or proposed assignment and shall pay to the Franchisor an Assignment Fee in the amount equal to ten percent (10%) of the initial franchise fee charged by the Franchisor in granting new franchises, the payment of which shall be a condition of the Franchisor granting consent to the assignment.

There will always be a fee for assignment. (Assignees rarely, if ever, have to pay a new initial franchise fee.) The amount is usually between $3,000 and $15,000. As in the example noted above, it is sometimes expressed as a percentage of the then current initial franchise fee charged by the franchisor in granting new franchises. This means that as the initial franchise fee goes up, so too does the assignment fee. Some franchisors justify the assignement fee as it is meant to compensate the franchisor for its training (unless there is a separate training fee to be paid). A separate training fee is becoming more prevalent in addition to an assignment fee.

You are required to pay the assignment fee, but it may be something that you are obtaining through the purchase price from the assignee.

10.5   Right of First Refusal

(a)   Prior to granting consent to any proposed assignment, the Franchisor shall have a right of first refusal to purchase the Franchised Business from the Franchisee.

> The Franchisee shall notify the Franchisor of its desire to sell, assign, or transfer the Franchised Business by written notice setting forth the proposed terms and conditions for such sale, assignment, or transfer. The Franchisor shall then notify the Franchisee in writing within fourteen (14) days after receipt of such notice as to whether or not the Franchisor wishes to exercise its right of first refusal on such terms and conditions.

This right of first refusal allows the franchisor to purchase the franchised business from you before you can sell to a third party. Essentially, you must offer the business for sale to the franchisor first, and if the franchisor declines its right to purchase, then you are able to sell it on the open market, subject to the franchisor's approval of the new franchisee.

> (b)   If the Franchisor determines not to exercise its right of first refusal at that time, then the Franchisor may assist the Franchisee to find a suitable buyer from among those prospective Franchisees with whom the Franchisor has been in contact. If within the said 14-day period the Franchisor has not been able to assist the Franchisee, then the Franchisee may commence its efforts to sell the Franchised Business; provided, however, that the Franchisee shall submit all proposed advertisements for the sale of the Franchised Business to the Franchisor for its reasonable prior written approval as to form.

Here, the franchisor wishes to ensure that any advertising by one of its franchisees for the sale of a franchise business is done appropriately, and without misrepresentation or hyperbole.

> (c)   Once the Franchisee receives a bona fide offer to purchase from a third party, the Franchisee shall deliver written notice to the Franchisor setting forth all of the terms and conditions of the proposed sale and all available information concerning the proposed assignee, as well as a statutory declaration of the Franchisee or an officer thereof attaching a true and complete copy of the offer. The Franchisor shall have the right to communicate directly with the offeror. Within fourteen (14) days after the Franchisor's receipt of such notice and information, the Franchisor shall notify the Franchisee in writing as to whether or not it will exercise its right of first refusal on the same terms and conditions, or if not, whether or not it consents or does not consent to the proposed sale and assignment of this Agreement to the proposed assignee, together with any reasonable conditions of the Franchisor's consent, or the reasons for the Franchisor's non-consent.

A franchisee may normally wish to sell its franchise within the initial term or the renewal term. He or she may not wish to be in the business anymore or may determine that the price is right to sell and move on to other things such as retirement.

If you are in this situation, you cannot simply advertise the business and expect the franchisor will agree to your selection of an assignee. The franchisor will likely wish to review any advertisements made in newspapers or other media in terms of what is represented by you. As well, the franchisor may determine that it wishes to buy the franchised business and this provision allows it to do so at the price offered by a buyer. This is a first right of refusal provision whereby if you get a bona fide offer, then the franchisor can match that offer and acquire the business for itself. This is quite normal and not something to be negotiated.

10.6 Transfer of Shares of Corporate Franchisee

If the Franchisee (or part of the Franchisee) is a corporation, partnership, or other entity, a transfer, purchase back, or issuance of shares, or partnership or other interests, or any other transaction or series of transactions involving the same that would affect twenty-five percent (25%) or more of, or which would result in a change in control of the majority of the voting or equity interests in the Franchisee directly or indirectly shall constitute an assignment for the purposes of this Agreement and shall require the Franchisor's consent pursuant to this Agreement. The directors, officers, shareholders, or partners and their voting and equity interests in the Franchisee as at the effective date of this Agreement are as stated in Schedule "A" to this Agreement.

This provision simply provides that the franchisor must consent to any transfer of shares of 25 percent or more, or which would result in a "change of control" of the principals who own the franchised business. A person should not be able to transfer his or her interest in the franchise indirectly without consent if consent is required for a direct transfer. This is reasonably standard.

10.7 Death or Incapacity of the Franchisee

In the event of the death or permanent incapacity or disability of the Franchisee or of the sole or main principal thereof in which the Franchisee is a corporation or other entity with only one or one main principal thereof active in the day-to-day management and operation of the Franchised Business, the Franchisee or its estate shall have the right to assign this Agreement within ninety (90) days, subject to the Franchisor's conditions of assignment provided in this Article 10. Otherwise, the Franchisee or its estate shall appoint a full-time manager for the Franchised Business reasonably satisfactory to the Franchisor who shall be required to complete the Franchisor's training program. The Franchisor reserves the right to charge a fee of no more than $1,000 to train any untrained manager so appointed by the estate. For the purposes of this Agreement, permanent incapacity or disability shall mean inability to attend to the day-to-day business operations of the Franchised Business for a material part of the normal working day for a period of three (3) months or more. In the event of any such death or permanent incapacity or disability, the Franchisor may provide reasonable assistance to the Franchisee or its estate to find a suitable buyer or manager for the Franchised Business, but the Franchisor has the right to charge a fee of no more than $5,000 for any sale to a third party arranged or brokered by the Franchisor.

It is not inconceivable that the principal operator of a franchised business could become disabled or could die during the course of operation of the business. Who then takes over the business? If the business is operated by a husband and wife, and the wife owns some interest in the franchised business, then it is likely that the franchisor will consent to the wife continuing with her ownership and operation of the business after the husband's death. The problem occurs when there is no spouse or adult children that are prepared to run the business upon the death or disability of the principal operator, or the spouse and children of the now deceased or disabled principal operator are deemed to be inadequate or incapable of running the business.

There should at least be some provision made that would allow the franchisee or the estate to have some time to sell the franchised business in order to safeguard the franchisee's investment in it.

Here, the franchisor has the right to appoint a manager to run the franchised business, to charge the franchisee for training or retraining of management personnel, and to assist the franchising corporation to find a suitable buyer for the franchised business. As this normally takes time and administrative assistance by the franchisor's office, the franchisor normally charges a fee for brokering a sale in these circumstances.

13

DEFAULT AND TERMINATION

As a prospective franchisee, you should be aware of the section in the franchise agreement that deals with default and termination. You need to be aware of the following matters that entitle the franchisor to default and perhaps terminate your agreement.

11. DEFAULT AND TERMINATION

11.1 No Encumbrance of Franchise

The Franchisee shall not have the right to pledge, encumber, charge, hypothecate, or otherwise give any third party a security interest in this Agreement without the prior written consent of the Franchisor, such consent not to be reasonably withheld. The Franchisor will be entitled to withhold its consent in circumstances where such pledge, encumbrance, charge, or hypothecation is, in the Franchisor's reasonable opinion, being done for purposes other than for conventional loans or bank financings, equipment leasing, or equipment or inventory purchasing.

You are not permitted to grant a security interest, chattel mortgage, or other charge on the business assets of the franchise without the franchisor's consent, but such consent cannot be withheld in circumstances in which you are simply obtaining a conventional loan from a bank or leasing company. Normally, the bank will want to have a first priority on the assets it is loaning money to you for. As a commercial reality, franchisors may wish to take security on those assets as well, but their priority would be second or subsequent to the bank.

11.2 Effect of Seizure or Insolvency

In the event of the termination of this Agreement for any reason, no assignee for the benefit of creditors, receiver, receiver-manager, trustee in bankruptcy, liquidator, sheriff, bailiff, or other officer of the Court or official charged with taking over custody of the Franchisee's assets, inventory, or business shall have any right to assume and continue to perform under this Agreement.

A clause such as this won't necessarily prevent a trustee or receiver from taking over the business; lawyers put clauses like this in franchise agreements just in case it works, denying a trustee or receiver the right to own, operate, and sell to another franchisee. A good point to remember is this: just because it's in the agreement doesn't mean it's going to be enforceable.

11.3 Rectification of Defaults

The Franchisee shall promptly rectify all defaults or failures to perform any of its obligations (which are, by their nature, capable of curing) under this Agreement upon receipt of written notice from the Franchisor specifying the default or failure and the requirements to cure such default or failure.

Usually, franchise agreements will separate out curable from non-curable defaults. Curable defaults may be defaults that may be cured simply by the payment of money or the taking of certain steps within a particular time period (e.g., seven or ten days' notice to cure a financial default such as non-payment of royalties). There may be room for you to negotiate extensions to curing periods in which such curing periods are unreasonable or inadequate (e.g., you are granted one day to cure financial defaults, is it possible to expand this to three or five?).

It should be recognized that some defaults, by their very nature, may well be practically incurable such as a landlord seizing the goods of the franchisee tenant; a bankruptcy or receivership, or other such events.

Unless they are patently unreasonable, I tend to leave the default provisions alone for the same reason I don't negotiate the interest on the late payments clause. Negotiating interest on late payments may suggest you intend to be a late payer. Negotiating standard boilerplate default provisions suggests you might regularly be in default. A franchise lawyer may well be able to advise you what is standard in the industry. Certainly, 7 to 14 days to cure a monetary default is reasonably standard, although I have seen 21 and 30 days in some agreements.

11.4 Termination after Notice of Default

The Franchisor may terminate this Agreement after written notice of default setting forth the Franchisor's intent to terminate, the reasons for such termination, and the effective date thereof, as follows:

(a)   If the Franchisee fails to comply with the Franchisor's specifications, and standards for services, inventory, and supplies, as called for in this Agreement or in the Operations Manual and such default shall not be wholly rectified within a period of seven (7) days after written notice, specifying such default, shall be given by the Franchisor to the Franchisee;

The franchisor can terminate you with notice to cure (as per Section **11.4** above) or without any notice at all (as per Section **11.5** below). The grounds for termination in Section **11.4** are not extensive. Simply, if you fail to comply with the franchisor's specifications and have not cured such default within seven days, you can be terminated. In reality, the default has to be serious, fundamental, and even regular or the courts will be reluctant to enforce the termination. (See section **d.** below.)

(b)   If the Franchisee operates the Franchised Business in a dishonest, illegal, unsafe, unsanitary, or unethical manner, or engages in any conduct related to the Franchised Business that in the Franchisor's reasonable opinion materially and adversely affects or may affect the reputation, identification, and image of the EMMA & JEREMY'S System or Trade-marks, for a period of seven (7) days after written notice, specifying such default and such time period for curing such default, shall be given by the Franchisor to the Franchisee;

(c)   If the Franchisee fails to pay any amount due and owing to the Franchisor or an approved supplier pursuant to the terms of this Agreement (including, but without limitation, payments in respect of Continuing Royalties or the Advertising Fund) for a period of seven (7) days after written notice, specifying such default and such time period for curing such default, shall be given by the Franchisor to the Franchisee; or

If you have failed to pay a required amount, such as continuing royalties, or contributions towards the advertising fund within 7 days, the franchisor may terminate.

(d)   The Franchisee fails to comply with any othe oblgation under this Agreement for a period of thirty (30) days after written notice, specifying such default and such time period for curing such default, shall be given by the Franchisor to the Franchisee.

If you fail to comply with any other obligations, within 30 days of notice, the franchisor may terminate.

As suggested above, the reality is that courts are reluctant to terminate franchise rights in circumstances in which the default under the agreement is not "material." You have invested hundreds of thousands of dollars in the operation of the franchised business and may lose all your investment (and your house) if terminated. For example, a failure by you to use green garbage cans instead of yellow ones may well breach the franchise agreement, the operations manual, and the standards set by the franchisor, but is displaying the wrong coloured garbage cans a material breach upon which a franchisor would be prepared to terminate you? Normally, successful terminations occur in circumstances in which you have not only failed to comply with certain fundamental aspects of the system, but have also failed to pay money as and when due. The case law in each province differs; if you are in this situation, you should be assessing your position with your franchise lawyer.

Franchisors will usually build a file outlining various defaults before acting on termination. You are advised to ensure that you are up to date at all times in respect of royalties, advertising fund contributions, and other monies due and owing. But if you keep getting notices of default from the franchisor, this could indicate that a file is being built up in support of termination. If you believe that a default has been cured, or the default has been a misunderstanding due to some prior agreement with the franchisor, then you should answer each and every default letter by a response to the franchisor in writing. Build your own file with the knowledge that the franchisor is building its own file as well.

There will often be a provision that states that the franchisor may terminate if you have received three defaults within the last 12-month period. Although this may appear in many franchise agreements, even where there is no such clause, franchisors rarely hang their hat on one default. This is because the court may view the default as not material enough to justify termination. It may not be sufficient or material enough grounds to cause a judge to agree that the default justified termination.

To reiterate, if the franchisor is building a case to support termination, you should respond at every opportunity indicating that you are in compliance, have paid the money, or otherwise did not breach the franchise agreement (assuming that this is the case and that you are in compliance, didn't breach the agreement, and don't owe the money).

11.5   Termination without Prior Notice of Default

The following events shall be deemed material breaches of this Agreement and shall be grounds for termination of this Agreement by the Franchisor without prior notice of default. Such material breaches shall, by their nature, be deemed non-curable. Any notice of termination given by the Franchisor to the Franchisee upon or after the happening of any of such events shall be in writing and shall set forth the Franchisor's reasons for such termination and the effective date thereof. The events of non-curable material breach of this Agreement are as follows:

(a)   If the Franchisee shall abandon the Franchised Business by failing to keep the Franchised Business operating under the name EMMA & JEREMY'S for five (5) consecutive business days or more, or for an aggregate of five (5) business days or more in any 30-day period, without the prior written consent of the Franchisor, which consent shall not be unreasonably withheld where the closure results from a cause beyond the Franchisee's reasonable control;

(b)   If the Franchisee shall become bankrupt, or be in receivership for a period exceeding ten (10) days, or shall be dissolved, liquidated, or wound-up, or if the Franchisee shall make a general assignment for the benefit of its creditors or a composition, arrangement or proposal involving its creditors, or otherwise acknowledge its insolvency;

(c)   If the Franchisee, or any partner, director, or officer shall be charged or convicted of any misdemeanor, or shall be found liable for or guilty of fraud, fraudulent conversion, embezzlement, or any comparable action in any civil or criminal action or proceeding pertaining or relevant in the Franchisor's opinion to the Franchised Business;

Note the use of the term "misdemeanor," which is an American concept with no specific equivalent in Canadian criminal law. This would be an example of a US franchise agreement being adapted for use in Canada, but not adapted particularly well. You may see the word "felony" in a US-style agreement that also has no legal meaning in Canada. Although we've all see enough TV to remember that a felony is a serious criminal offence, I never correct these mistakes. When there are clear mistakes in the franchise agreement caused by the franchisor making reference to the wrong statute, the wrong body of law, or a foreign concept (e.g., felony) it is suggested here that you not raise the issue and not negotiate it.

By correcting the franchisor's mistakes you are simply making the agreement more enforceable against you, where it might not otherwise have been. A franchisor trying to terminate you because it believes you have been convicted of a misdemeanor will have a big surprise when it's discovered that aspect of the agreement has no counterpart in Canada and will be unenforceable.

(d)   If the Franchisee shall be convicted of misleading advertising or any other sales-related statutory offence pertaining to the Franchised Business, or shall be enjoined from or ordered to cease operating the Franchised Business by reason of dishonest, illegal, unsafe, unsanitary, or unethical conduct;

While I believe unethical franchisees should be terminated, this may be hard to substantiate. It may take years for these statutory offenses to make their way to trial, delaying termination if a conviction occurs.

> (e) If the Franchisee shall have its business license or any other license, permit, or registration pertaining to the Franchised Business or the Franchised Location suspended for just cause or cancelled and not reinstated or re-issued within ten (10) business days;
>
> (f) If the Franchisee shall attempt to pledge, encumber, charge, hypothecate, or otherwise give any third party a security interest in, or assign this Agreement without the prior written consent of the Franchisor, or if an assignment of this Agreement shall occur by operation of law or judicial process without such consent;
>
> (g) If the Franchisee shall attempt to assign, transfer, or convey the Trade-marks, trade name, copyrights, confidential information, or trade secrets, or if the Franchisee shall publish, disclose, or use any of the same in a manner or at or from a location not authorized by the Franchisor;
>
> (h) If the Franchisee shall intentionally falsify, misrepresent, or misstate to the Franchisor any financial statements, reports, or information required pursuant to this Agreement;
>
> (i) If the Franchisee shall fail to develop the Franchised Location Premises in the time agreed by the Franchisee and the Franchisor for such development; or

Where does the money go that you have paid if the franchisor purports to rely on this clause?

> (j) If the Franchisee shall unilaterally repudiate this Agreement or the performance or observance of any of the terms and conditions of this Agreement by word or conduct evidencing the Franchisee's intention to no longer comply with or be bound by the same.

This provision is normally in respect of circumstances in which the franchisee has "walked away" from the business or taken down the signs to operate a competing business or has become bankrupt, or other events that are difficult if not impossible to cure.

You will note that some provisions have a curing period. This allows you to overturn the bankruptcy petition or argue your case in court (with respect to why the receivership or bankruptcy should not apply).

A material breach shall entitle the Franchisor to take whatever steps it deems appropriate in the circumstances.

The franchisor may not have the resources or the desire to terminate you. By terminating you, the franchisor is opening itself up to expensive legal proceedings that might last a number of years.

Franchisor/franchisee disputes, if taken to court, could cost the franchisor several tens of thousands of dollars in legal fees (that's a low estimate) and the franchisor might not be successful in all instances. The franchisor also may not have the resources to take over the franchised location and run it itself (it may have to undertake payment of the rent and the salaries of the existing or new employees).

Accordingly, even though the franchisor might be in a position to terminate the agreement, it might choose not to terminate at any particular time. Some agreements provide for the franchisor to take other action, such as reducing exclusivity in the territory (i.e., cancelling any exclusive territory that the franchisor has granted you and instead, allowing another location to be established in that former exclusive territory). The franchisor may also choose not to renew the franchise agreement as opposed to terminating it. That is, it might wait 14 months for the agreement to expire and simply not renew based on your defaults. Where a franchisor has a number of outstanding defaults against you and is not taking steps to terminate, non-renewal may be on the agenda.

11.6 Cross Default

Where there is more than one agreement or other instrument in existence between the Franchisee and the Franchisor or the Franchisee and an affiliate of the Franchisor (as the term affiliate is defined in the British Columbia *Company Act*), the Franchisee agrees that the Franchisor has the right to treat a material breach or default of any one agreement or instrument as a material breach or default of all or any of the other agreements or instruments, and any such material breach or default of any one agreement or instrument shall be treated, in respect of any of the other agreements or instruments, as a material breach or default of each such agreement or instrument in accordance with its own terms.

In addition to the specific default and termination provisions, many franchise agreements also contain "cross default" provisions. Normally, in situations in which there is more than one agreement being entered into between the franchisor and you, such as both a franchise agreement and a sublease, a cross default clause is intended to make a default of any one of the agreements a default of all of them.

If you are in a situation in which you have more than one franchise location with the same franchisor, these clauses must be looked at to see whether the effects of the clause would extend further to make a default of one franchise by you into a default of both (or all) of the franchises. If this appears to be the way the cross default clause is worded, it may be something that can be negotiated with the franchisor when more than one franchise purchase is being contemplated, in order to have each franchise stand on its own and remain unaffected by defaults occurring in a different franchise (e.g., if one fails, the others can still survive).

11.7   Right of the Franchisor to Repurchase

(a)   Upon expiry or termination of this Agreement for whatever reason, the Franchisor shall have the option, exercisable by notice in writing to the Franchisee within thirty (30) days of expiry or termination, to purchase from the Franchisee all or any of the following items upon the following terms:

    (i)   inventory and supplies, other than damaged, obsolete, or discontinued items, at a price equal to the Franchisee's invoiced cost;

    (ii)   leasehold improvements, equipment, fixtures, and furnishings, at a price equal to the then current fair market value thereof; and

    (iii)   assignments of the leases for items leased (but not leased from the Franchisor) for a consideration equal to the amount, if any, of the prepaid benefits then existing under any such leases.

In circumstances in which the franchisor has terminated you (or the franchise agreement has expired without renewal), you may have equipment, assets, and inventory located at the premises, which you may not be able to utilize because it is proprietary, it bears the franchisor's trade-mark, or it is only suited to the particular franchise business in question.

The franchisor may also need this equipment to operate the business in the event of termination. You cannot "strip the premises down" and take everything that you own. This is because the franchise agreement normally contains an "option to purchase" provision, whereby the franchisor has the right to purchase such equipment, assets, and inventory for a price as indicated in the franchise agreement.

Note that the franchisor does not have the obligation to purchase the equipment, assets, or inventory. It can "cherry pick" what it wants. The price is usually determined to be the fair market value as determined by an independent appraisal.

(b)   If the parties cannot reasonably agree upon the then current fair market value, it shall be determined by an independent appraisal, and the costs of appraisal shall be borne equally by the parties;

If the franchised business has been terminated, or the franchised rights have expired, then the business is no longer a "going concern." If it is no longer a going concern under the franchisor's trade-mark and system, then arguably the assets are worth far less than what they might be if the business was appraised on a going concern basis.

In other words, if the franchisor terminates you and seeks to repurchase the assets from you, the appraiser may be instructed to appraise the value of the assets on their value being sold as piecemeal as opposed to their value within the franchised business. If the definition of fair market value in this option to purchase clause prescribes that the assets would be priced on the bases of fair market value with the business operating as a going concern, this might conceivably yield more money for you. However, you should be realistic. After a number of years, the value of restaurant or retail equipment is small.

(c) The Franchisor shall in each instance be entitled to deduct from any monies payable to the Franchisee pursuant to the aforesaid options any and all sums of money due and owing by the Franchisee to the Franchisor (or its affiliates) and then remaining unpaid, and whether under this Agreement or any other instrument or agreement then in existence between the Franchisee and the Franchisor; and

Note also that the franchisor has a right of set off. Set off allows the franchisor to buy the franchised business's assets at fair market value (whatever that turns out to be), but instead of paying you that amount, the franchisor can apply it to any debts owed to it by you. This will reduce the amount of money the franchisor would be entitled to claim.

(d) The Franchisor shall be entitled to assign any or all of its said options to purchase to a successor Franchisee or to any other party.

11.8   Telephone Numbers and Listings

Upon expiry or termination of this Agreement for whatever reason, the Franchisor shall have the right to require that the Franchisee forthwith upon written notice to cease use of all of the existing telephone numbers (including fax numbers) for the Franchised Business. The Franchisor shall have the further right to arrange for call forwarding and to take over and have assigned to it or its designee the existing telephone numbers and directory listings for the Franchised Business;

It may be that notwithstanding this clause, the telephone company will take the position that it is their telephone number, and they're not prepared to assign it to anyone unless it's on their standard assignment form, and signed in triplicate. Power of attorney clauses are sometimes included within this "assignment of telephone number" provision allowing the franchisor to sign the documents as the franchisee's attorney in fact.

11.9 No Removal of Assets

During the term and currency of this Agreement, and both before and after notice of default, except with the prior written consent of the Franchisor, the Franchisee shall not remove all or any substantial part of its business assets (particularly, its inventory of food products used in operating the Franchised Business from the Franchised Location premises). The Franchisee hereby acknowledges and agrees that such business assets shall be retained at the Franchised Location premises and shall be and remain charged hereby with a continuing collateral security interest in favour of the Franchisor for all monies due and accruing due and owing by the Franchisee to the Franchisor under or pursuant to this Agreement from time to time.

This clause has been inserted in the franchise agreement as some protection to the franchisor that you will not engage in a "midnight run" and remove business assets in the middle of the night (or day).

Note as well in this clause, the franchise agreement creates a security interest in the business assets of the premises. Normally, you will be required to sign a general security agreement in favor of the franchisor on a separate document. In some franchise agreements, there is no separate security agreement, but a security interest is created within the franchise agreement, as it is here. Most provinces under the *Personal Property Security Act* (PPSA) provide for a good faith obligation, which may be of assistance in those provinces without specific franchise legislation (although a common-law duty of good faith seems to have been recognized by our courts).

11.10 The Franchisee's Obligations of Discontinuance upon Termination

Upon expiration or termination of this Agreement for whatever reason, the Franchisee shall forthwith discontinue use of the Trade-marks, trade name, copyrights, computer software, Operations Manual, confidential information, and trade secrets, and shall not thereafter operate or do business under any name or in any manner that might tend to give the general public the impression that it is, either directly or indirectly, associated, affiliated, licensed by, or related to the Franchisor or the EMMA & JEREMY'S System and shall not, either directly or indirectly, use any trade-mark, name, logo, slogan, copyright, trade secret, confidential information, advertising, design, graphic, script, trade dress, colour combination, distinguishing feature, or other element that is confusingly similar to or colourably imitative of those used by the EMMA & JEREMY'S System. The Franchisee acknowledges the proprietary rights as set out in this Agreement and agrees to forthwith return to the Franchisor all copies in its possession of the Operations Manual, and all other confidential and proprietary information and materials relating to the EMMA & JEREMY'S System or bearing the Trade-marks. The covenants of this paragraph shall also extend to cover and bind each director, officer, and principal of the Franchisee who has in any capacity affixed his or her signature to this Agreement.

This provision obliges you to cease use of the franchisor's system and trade-marks at the conclusion of the term (whether the term has been ended by way of termination or expiration).

More often than not, upon termination or expiration of the franchise agreement, the franchisee will stop being an Emma & Jeremy's Donut Emporium and Internet Café franchise because the franchisee will no longer have title to the premises. The franchisor will have terminated the sublease at the same time the franchisor would have terminated the franchise agreement (or the two would expire together) leaving the franchisee without the premises. In some cases, however, the franchisee will remain on the premises because it is the tenant under its own lease, and the lease still has time to run. But the franchise agreement will normally contain a restrictive covenant preventing the former franchisee from being in the donut and Internet café business.

11.11 Indemnification

Except as expressly provided elsewhere in this Agreement, the Franchisee agrees to save the Franchisor and its respective directors and officers harmless from and to indemnify it and them against all claims, demands, actions, causes of action, suits, proceedings, judgments, settlements, debts, losses, damages, costs, charges, fines, penalties, assessments, taxes, liens, liabilities, and expenses, including legal fees and disbursements and costs of any action, suit or proceeding on a solicitor and his or her own client basis, of whatever kind or character arising out of or incurred as a result of or in connection with any breach, default, violation, repudiation or non-performance of this Agreement by the Franchisee, or any act or error of omission or commission on the part of the Franchisee or anyone for whom the Franchisee is responsible in law, or on account of any actual or alleged loss, injury, or damage to any person, firm, or corporation or to any property in any way arising out of, resulting from, or connected with the Franchisee's business conducted pursuant to this Agreement.

An indemnification is a covenant similar to a guarantee. One party protects another party from any claims, demands, actions, or other forms of legal proceedings against such other party that may have arisen owing to the fault, action, or inaction of the other party.

In this case, the franchisee indemnifies the franchisor and its directors, officers, etc., from all actions or claims initiated by third parties against the franchisor in respect to the franchisee's operation of the business.

By way of example, if a customer suffers a bout of food poisoning and attributes that food poisoning to eating at your restaurant, the customer could sue you for his or her damages. The customer will likely, however, sue the franchisor as well, even though the customer has no contract with the franchisor and even though you are an independent contractor to the franchisor. The franchisor will still be brought into the inevitable litigation, and although the franchisor will, in this example, likely face no liability, it will still have legal expenses to pay arising from something you did or did not do. The indemnity will allow the franchisor to make a claim against you for such expenses.

11.12 Non-Competition

(a) The Franchisee and its principal operators as indicated on Schedule "A" shall not, during the term and currency of this Agreement, directly or indirectly, in any capacity whatsoever, compete with the Franchised Business that is the subject matter of this Agreement by way of owning or operating, whether directly or indirectly, a similar business to that represented by the EMMA & JEREMY'S System;

(b) The covenants of this paragraph shall continue to apply to the Franchisee and the persons specified in Schedule "A" hereof and shall survive any assignment or transfer of this Agreement, or the expiration or termination of this Agreement, for a period of five (5) years, and during such time shall be applicable at the Franchised Location and within a radius of twenty-five (25) kilometres of the Franchised Location, and twenty-five (25) kilometres from any other EMMA & JEREMY'S INTERNET CAFÉ & DONUT EMPORIUM then established;

A restrictive covenant (also know as a non-competition clause) is an agreement by a person or company not to compete with another person or company for a period of time. By way of example, the franchisor has trained you and has allowed you to operate the franchised business and utilize the franchisor's business system for some period of time. If you were to remove all signs, stop paying royalties, and start carrying on the identical business under your own name, the franchisor's legitimate business interests are threatened.

Courts have allowed franchisors to restrict competition from the franchisee under certain circumstances. As the law does not like to restrain trade or competition, restrictive covenants such as this will only be enforceable if they are reasonable and the law has evolved such that restrictive covenants are only reasonable if they protect the franchisor's interests both geographically and in terms of time and that the restriction itself is reasonable. A restrictive covenant preventing the franchisee from operating a similar business within 25 kilometres of the franchised location will likely be unenforceable because it has no time element within the covenant.

Likewise, a restrictive covenant preventing you from competing with the franchisor for five years would likely be unenforceable because it has no geographic element. There normally has to be both and the nature of the restriction must be reasonable.

In the clause above, the franchisee is restricted from competing with the franchisor for a period of five years within a 25-kilometre radius of the franchised location, and any other location that the franchisor may have established at that time. This covenant may be unenforceable for two reasons.

First, the scope of the protection is arguably too large, and second, the time the franchisee must not be in the same or a similar business may be too long. Generally, covenants of two kilometres and two years will be enforceable in Canada, but here the covenant is for five years and 25 kilometres. Such a covenant would effectively keep the franchisee out of the same business within an entire city for half a decade.

It is suggested here that if a covenant looks unenforceable, you should not try to point this out to the franchisor only to make it enforceable. That is, if the franchisor's lawyers have made an error by drafting a restrictive covenant that is either too long or too broad, don't try to reduce the length of time or scope of the restrictive covenant because by doing so you may be making an unenforceable covenant enforceable.

There is another problem with this covenant. Note in the above clause, the franchisee is prevented from operating a business "similar" to the EMMA & JEREMY'S System. It is suggested here that the description may render the covenant imprecise and therefore unenforceable. What is the EMMA & JEREMY'S System? It's a lot of things in this agreement, but is it donuts, or is it donuts in conjunction with an Internet café? If a franchisor seeks to make its restrictive covenant enforceable, then the franchisor should specifically indicate what the franchisee is precluded from doing. Operating a business "similar to that of the franchisors" will not be specific enough to satisfy the courts. This clause is potentially unenforceable for the reasons noted above.

You will also see a restrictive covenant that is drafted in such a way that the territory in which the franchisee cannot compete seems to expand with every clause (i.e., if not five kilometres, then four kilometres, if not four kilometres, then three kilometres). Courts have scrutinized this form of "concentric circle drafting" and some Canadian courts are not fond of it. Such provisions may also be unenforceable.

(c)   The covenants of this paragraph shall also extend to cover and bind each director, officer, and principal of the Franchisee who has in any capacity affixed his or her signature to this Agreement;

You will note that the restrictive covenant seeks to bind all directors, officers, and principals of the franchisee. Because there is not "privity of contract" between the franchisor and these other persons, it is doubtful that the agreement would be enforceable against a director or an officer of the franchisee company unless those persons actually executed the agreement in their personal capacities.

A franchise lawyer will give you a better sense of whether or not a restrictive covenant such as this is likely to be enforceable.

> (d)   The covenants of this paragraph shall not operate to prevent the Franchisee or such other persons from being involved in the restaurant business generally following expiration or termination of this Agreement, but shall operate so as to have the effect of preventing the Franchisee and such other persons from being involved in the business in any way, directly or indirectly, which utilizes the essential distinctive elements belonging to the EMMA & JEREMY'S System as detailed in this Agreement and serving Oriental foods; and

There is a deliberate error in this clause, but it may be accidental in your form of agreement. The reference to "Oriental" foods indicates that the precedent that the franchisor or its lawyer used when preparing this agreement was presumably based on a Chinese or Japanese food concept. What is it doing in a donut franchise agreement? The mistake illustrates the problem of old legal precedents, demanding schedules, and bad proofing. Sometimes, lawyers are careless. Sometimes, the franchisor has drawn the agreement up itself and has not used a lawyer (but has found this great Chinese food agreement that they use as a template for this donut concept). Unfortunately they may have missed a few references from the former concept, failing to remove all references to Chinese food; totally inapplicable to the franchise agreement at issue. The result? You win!

> (e)   The Franchisor reserves the right at any time upon written notice to the Franchisee to that effect to unilaterally curtail, reduce, or limit any provision of this Section 11.13, and the parties agree to be bound by and perform the same as so modified from time to time.

11.13 No Solicitation of Customers, Employees, Suppliers, or the Franchisees

The Franchisee shall not attempt to obtain any unfair advantage either during the Term of this Agreement or thereafter by soliciting or attempting to induce any customer, employee, supplier, or Franchisee of the Franchisor to divert his or her business, employment, or contract to the Franchisee or any other competitive business, by the use of customer, supplier or Franchisee lists or employee information derived from the Franchisee's knowledge of and association and experience with the Franchised Business and the EMMA & JEREMY'S System during the term hereof, and the Franchisee acknowledges that all such customer and supplier lists constitute confidential information and are trade secrets belonging to the EMMA & JEREMY'S System. The covenants of this paragraph shall also extend to cover and bind each director, officer, and principal of the Franchisee who has in any capacity affixed his or her signature to this Agreement, including those persons specified in Schedule "A."

This clause prevents the franchisee from hiring away the franchisor's employees, or the employees of other franchisees in the franchisee's new business. The provision is reasonable to protect the franchisor's business interests and is not something that would be negotiated.

Leave these sorts of motherhood clauses alone. Why would you want to hire away the franchisor's staff after termination anyway?

11.14 Injunctive Relief

The Franchisor may bring action for injunctive relief in order to compel the Franchisee to comply with its obligations under this Agreement so as to preserve and protect the Trademarks and other proprietary rights under this Agreement and to maintain the uniformity and integrity of the EMMA & JEREMY'S System as called for under this Agreement. Where such elements are involved, the Franchisee agrees that the balance of convenience between the parties in any such action rests with the Franchisor, who in obtaining any such injunctive relief shall not be required to post any bond or other security.

As noted above, the franchisor does not necessarily have to terminate you upon a material, or any other, default. The franchisor may instead choose to compel you to comply with the mandatory elements of the system and obtain a court order to do so. Be advised that in agreements such as this in which you are agreeing in advance to the "balance of convenience" on the side of the franchisor, such provisions are, generally speaking, unenforceable. The court will determine this.

The court might also order you to comply with the injunction and pay royalties until trial; 18 months down the road. Perhaps there are better ways to resolve disputes than litigation.

11.15 Mediation

The parties agree that any dispute, other than an action brought by the Franchisor for injunctive relief as set forth in Section 11.15 above, and other than a claim of Franchisor relating to preserving and protecting the Trade-marks and other proprietary rights under this Agreement or to maintaining the uniformity and integrity of the System as called for under this Agreement or to specific sums of money owed by the Franchisee to the Franchisor under or pursuant to this Agreement, shall be submitted promptly to non-binding mediation upon the agreement of both parties hereby given. Mediation shall be before a single skilled independent mediator and held in a location mutually and reasonably agreed upon by the parties, and the costs of mediation shall be borne equally by the parties.

Mediation is often a successful means of resolving disputes, especially where the parties have an ongoing relationship such as a franchise relationship. Mediation occurs when an independent third party assists the parties in resolving their dispute (rather than a court or arbitrator making that determination for the parties). It is possible (and desirable) that the parties choose someone with some understanding of franchising or the industry the franchisor and franchisee are in (i.e., the restaurant industry) to act as a mediator. Various bodies act as appointing authorities by finding a mediator with knowledge of the area.

Mediation is usually voluntary and always non-binding. If a skilled independent mediator can help the parties to reach a settlement agreement, the dispute is over, and often this can be achieved amicably. If no compromise agreement can be reached to settle the dispute by mediation, the mediation process will not force a settlement on the parties. Instead, the result will be that the status quo remains, and the parties are left in the same positions they were in before the mediation. In order to settle the dispute, they must then move on to arbitration or litigation. If this occurs, it is often possible for at least some of the disputed issues to be resolved by mediation, which would result in a lesser number of issues being left to resolve by arbitration or litigation, at a potentially lower cost to both parties.

Remember, mediators must be paid. It's a cost normally divided equally between the parties. In my experience, mediation works well to solve ongoing franchisor/franchisee disputes without ten-day trials booked two years in advance, and without the high cost of litigation counsel.

11.16 Arbitration

If no agreement is reached as a result of such mediation process, then the parties agree that any such dispute shall be submitted to arbitration upon the agreement of both parties, and in accordance with the provisions of the Commercial Arbitration legislation applicable to this Agreement. The arbitration shall be conducted according to the rules specified or mentioned in such legislation, failing which it shall be conducted according to such rules as the parties shall mutually and reasonably agree upon, failing which it shall be conducted according to such rules as the arbitrator or arbitrators shall specify or mutually and reasonably agree upon. Arbitration shall be before a single independent arbitrator, or if the parties cannot reasonably agree upon a single arbitrator, then before a board of three independent arbitrators, one appointed by each party and the third appointed by the other two arbitrators so appointed, and the decision of the arbitrator or a majority of the board of arbitrators as the case may be shall be final and binding upon the parties, and judgment upon the award may be entered and enforced in the same manner as a judgment or order of the Court to the same effect.

Arbitration is more formal than mediation, but less formal than court. Many franchise agreements will contain an arbitration clause, although little thought may have gone into the selection of the clause or its mechanics. Arbitration can be an extremely valuable means of dispute resolution. With the greatest respect to our courts, franchising is such a specialized area that many judges will have had little or no experience with it. This can be a disadvantage both to the franchisor and you.

Arbitration allows the parties to select an appropriate person to resolve the dispute with hopes that the person will have experience with franchising. Arbitration may also allow a more speedy resolution to a dispute rather than through the courts, where trial dates are 18 months to two years in the future if a judge is available at all.

The usual "panel of three" arbitrators provision may well give "lip service" to the principal of arbitration in franchising, but as a prospective franchisee, you must be aware that the costs of a panel of three are obviously three times higher than a panel of one. Can you afford to resolve a dispute by way of arbitration if a franchisor insists on a panel of three (whether it be because it does not approve of your choice of a single arbitrator, or simply for strategic reasons)? Can the franchise agreement be worded so as to restrict the arbitration to being before only one independent and mutually agreeable arbitrator?

Franchise agreement arbitration clauses will also normally contain a "carve out" provision, which allows the use of the courts for immediate injunctive relief such as when the franchisor's trade-marks (or its confidential information) are at risk.

Procedural rules are often simplified in arbitration and the arbitrator adopts his or her own procedure. The "judgment" may also remain confidential, if that is what the parties desire, in order that no precedent be set or the determination be of interest to nosey third parties (e.g., other franchisees).

Be aware that the arbitrator must be paid and the arbitrator may award costs against the losing party if that is what the agreement provides. It can be expensive, especially if three arbitrators are required to be appointed, because the parties can't agree on one person.

14

THE GUARANTEE AND GENERAL INFORMATION

12. GUARANTEE

12.1 Guarantee by Guarantor(s) of Franchisee's Obligations

In consideration of the Franchisor granting this franchise to the Franchisee, the Guarantor, hereby covenants and agrees to be personally bound by all of the terms and conditions of this Agreement as if the Guarantor were the Franchisee herein, and agrees that the Guarantor will, at all times, continually indemnify and hold harmless the Franchisor against any loss, damage, expense, liability, and cost that the Franchisor may sustain or incur by reason of any default of the Franchisee in the performance of the Franchisee's obligations or covenants contained in this Agrement, including, but without limitation, the payment of all monies payable to the Franchisor.

The Franchisor may, without the consent of the Guarantor, extend the time for payment of any monies payable hereunder or vary the terms of this Agreement as it, in its absolute discretion, deems necessary or advisable, but nevertheless, this covenant shall remain in full force and effect as a continuing guarantee and shall survive termination of the Franchisee and this Franchise Agreement.

The liability of the Guarantor to the Franchisor shall not be deemed to have been waived, released, discharged, impaired, or affected by reason of the release or discharge of the Franchisee in any receivership, bankruptcy, winding-up, or other creditor's proceeding, and shall continue with respect to the periods prior thereto and thereafter, for and with respect to the term of the franchise.

As the Guarantor is liable as a principal obligant under this Agreement, and not just as a surety, the Franchisor shall not be bound to exhaust its recourse against the Franchisee or other persons before being entitled to initiate action against or receive payment from the Guarantor in respect of the obligations of the Franchisee under this Agreement.

The liability of the Guarantor hereunder shall be joint and several with that of the Franchisee in respect of this Agreement and the guarantee of the Guarantor shall be absolute and unconditional. The Guarantor shall for all purposes of this guarantee and of this Agreement be regarded and be in the same position as a principal obligant and the Guarantor expressly waives demand, presentment, protest, and notice of default.

This guarantee and assumption of obligations shall be valid notwithstanding any change or changes in the name of the Franchisee or any change or changes in the owner-ship or control of the Franchisee corporation by death or by retirement of one or more of the officers or shareholders of such corporation, or by the introduction of new officers or shareholders, or an amalgamation of the Franchisee with any other corporation.

In the event there shall be more than one Guarantor, then the liability of the Guar-antors to the Franchisor shall be joint and several and notice to one Guarantor shall be deemed to be notice to all Guarantors. This guarantee and assumption of obligations on the part of the Guarantor shall extend to and enure to the benefit of the Franchisor, its successors and assigns.

The Guarantor shall not be entitled to any notices to the Franchisee as prescribed pursuant to Article 13 hereunder.

Franchisors will always seek to have a director or officer of the franchisee cor-poration guarantee the franchise agreement and any other obligation between franchisor and corporate franchisee.

Although there is no point to negotiating or modifying the wording of the guarantee, you may be able to limit the guarantee in the following ways:

- By having only one spouse, as opposed to both spouses, sign as guarantor. This could protect the other spouse's assets.

- Put a cap on the guarantee in terms of dollars. That is, the principal of the franchisee is liable to the franchisor for a fixed amount and no more (perhaps the amount of the initial franchise fee). The value in this is that you will know there's a personal obligation that will not exceed a certain amount if the franchised business is unsuccessful. Without a cap of this nature, the personal obligation of the franchisor may be substantial.

- Cap the guarantee in terms of years. Perhaps you could negotiate that the guarantee is removed after three years. The business will succeed or fail within 18 months. The franchisor might not need the guarantee in cir-cumstances in which it knows (after three years) that the franchise will be successful.

- Note that personal guarantees in Alberta must comply with the *Guarantees Acknowledgement Act* of Alberta and must be in a particular form and sworn before a notary or lawyer; otherwise, they are not enforceable.

13. GENERAL

13.1 Cumulative Remedies

The rights and remedies of the Franchisor are cumulative and no enforcement of a right or remedy shall preclude the enforcement of any other right or remedy.

13.2 Waiver

The Franchisor reserves the right from time to time to waive any of the obligations imposed under this Agreement on the Franchisee. No waiver by the Franchisor of any obligation or of any default or breach of any of the terms or conditions of this Agreement shall constitute a novation, or a waiver by the Franchisor of any other obligation, default, or breach.

A provision of the franchise agreement or the operations manual might be ignored by the franchisee and it might also be ignored by the franchisor. An example might be the requirement for the employees of the franchised business to wear uniforms. The franchisor might not have insisted upon uniforms and the franchisee has not acquired them for his or her employees. If the franchisor seeks to terminate the franchisee for its failure to insist upon uniforms to be worn by staff, the franchisor will be unsuccessful because it will have "waived" that part of the agreement. However, if it has waived a particular requirement for a period of time, it can put the franchisee on notice that it will no longer waive that requirement and in this case, the franchisee's employees will be required to wear uniforms if so directed by the franchisor.

13.3 Entire Agreement

This Agreement sets forth the entire understanding between the parties and contains all of the terms and conditions agreed upon by the parties with reference to the subject matter of this Agreement. No other agreements, oral or otherwise, shall be deemed to exist or to bind any of the parties, and all prior agreements and understandings are superseded hereby. No officer, employee, or agent of the Franchisor has any authority to make any agreement, warranty, representation, or promise not contained in this Agreement, and the Franchisee agrees that it has executed this Agreement without reliance upon any such agreement, warranty, representation, or promise.

This is an extremely important provision of any franchise agreement. This clause means that if there are any representations, warranties, or inducements made in the sales process, those warranties, representations, or inducements are no longer enforceable. The reason for this is because the "entire agreement" clause states that there are no prior representations or warranties and that all representations and warranties are in writing and part of the franchise agreement.

Accordingly, if the franchisor has provided all sorts of representations about sales and other matters and you wish to rely on such representations, they should be in writing and they should be part of the agreement, for example, within this agreement itself or as an addendum. However, you will find that franchisors are reluctant to incorporate any pre-contractual representation within the body of the agreement.

13.4 Recitals

The Recitals shall be included in and form a part of this Agreement.

13.5 Modification of Agreement

This Agreement may only be modified as expressly provided herein or otherwise by a written agreement signed by both the Franchisor and the Franchisee.

If there is an agreement between the parties to modify the franchise agreement (e.g., there has been an agreement to reduce the amount of advertising contributions required), then this amendment should be in writing and signed by both parties for it to be enforceable.

13.6 Covenant to Execute Further Documents or Acts

The parties agree to acknowledge, execute, and deliver all such further documents, instruments, or assurances and to perform all such further acts or deeds as may be reasonably required from time to time in order to carry out the terms and conditions of this Agreement in accordance with their true intent.

This provision obliges both parties to execute the documents that might not have been executed at the time of "closing" the transaction. Perhaps something has delayed the preparation of a trade-mark license agreement or equipment lease. You would be obliged to sign these documents even though presented with such documents well after the commencement of the franchised business if these documents were reasonably expected to be signed earlier. A trade-mark license is a good example of this.

13.7 Relationship of Parties

It is expressly agreed that the parties intend by this Agreement to establish the relationship of Franchisor and Franchisee, each as an independent contractor, and that it is not the intention of either party to establish a fiduciary or delegatory relationship or to undertake a partnership or joint venture or to make the Franchisee in any sense an agent, employee, beneficiary, co-venturer, or partner of the Franchisor. It is further agreed that the Franchisee has no authority to and will not transact any business or enter into any contract in the name of the Franchisor, or create or assume in the Franchisor's name or on its behalf in any manner, directly or indirectly, any liability or obligation, express or implied, or act or purport to act as its agent or representative for any purpose whatsoever, and the Franchisee shall not hold itself out as having any such authority, nor conduct itself in any manner so as to confuse, mislead, or deceive anyone as to its relationship with the Franchisor.

The franchisor does not want to be construed as an employer of the franchisee. It simply wants the relationship to be one of independent contractors. Accordingly, this clause provides that the franchisee is an independent contractor to the franchisor and not an employee, partner, or joint venturer, nor is there any "special" or fiduciary relationship between the franchisor and the franchisee. This is important because some regulatory bodies in Canada have found the franchisee to be a common employee of the franchisor. Franchisors desire to have no such designation or relationship with a franchisee other than independent contractual parties.

However, the more controlling the agreement is, the more the agreement resembles an employment agreement; and one day another government agency will take that position. So in many ways, it's in the franchisor's interest not to have a controlling and overbearing agreement.

13.8 Severability

In the event that any paragraph or sub-paragraph of this Agreement or any portion thereof shall be held to be indefinite, invalid, illegal, or otherwise void, voidable, or unenforceable, it shall be severed from this Agreement, and the balance of this Agreement shall continue in full force and effect.

13.9 Curtailment of Provisions

(a)   If any provision of this Agreement conflicts with any present or future law contrary to which the parties have no legal right to contract, or if any provision of this Agreement (other than for the payment of money) is deemed by any tribunal or Court to be unreasonable, the parties agree that the provision of this Agreement thus affected shall be curtailed and limited to the extent necessary to bring it within the requirements of the law or within what such tribunal or Court would have found to be reasonable in the circumstances, and this Agreement shall thus remain valid and enforceable, and the parties agree to be bound by and perform the same as so modified; and

(b)   The Franchisor reserves the right at any time upon written notice to the Franchisee to that effect to unilaterally curtail and limit any provision of this Agreement, and the parties agree to be bound by and perform the same as so modified from time to time.

If a provision of the agreement is deemed to be unenforceable or contrary to law, then the whole agreement is not unenforceable and the parties will construe the agreement to that effect.

13.10 Choice of Law

This Agreement shall be governed by and under the laws of the Province of Ontario, which the parties hereby choose to be the proper law of this agreement, and the parties agree to attorn to the jurisdiction of the courts in that Province.

Franchisors do not necessarily want to commence legal action and proceedings in your jurisdiction. Sometimes they want you to be forced into commencing legal proceedings in their jurisdiction. This can create considerable problems where the laws differ between the laws in your province and the laws in the province of the franchisor. This may also involve considerable extra expenses for you.

Here, the franchisor has chosen the laws of Ontario. This decision to make the laws of Ontario the governing law obliges the franchisor to comply with the *Wishart Act*, but what if the location is outside Ontario? Does the *Wishart Act* still apply? The law says no.

This type of clause is not only quite common, but also quite readily accepted by the courts as being something that the parties can "agree" to. Only in Alberta and Ontario, and other disclosure provinces, where the franchise legislation declares any choice of law or jurisdiction other than Alberta, Ontario, and other such provinces to be void in respect of claims enforceable under that franchise legislation, are these choices restricted by Canadian law.

In most of Canada, the general laws that would apply to most franchise lawsuits are not that different and so these clauses are not necessarily a bad thing in terms of the law, rather more a matter of the convenience or inconvenience and the expenses of the parties.

Another point to note is that many US-based franchisors wish to have the governing law and forum for all disputes to be under the laws of a particular US state, say, for example, Hawaii. The franchisor might be doing this because its head office is in Hawaii and it is familiar with the laws of Hawaii (ironically Hawaii's laws are among the toughest franchise laws in the United States).

The franchisor might also be choosing the laws of Hawaii to put the franchisee at economic disadvantage. It's a long way to go for a court application.

Canadian franchise lawyers usually recommend to their American clients to select a province in Canada as the governing law and forum for all disputes, particularly the law of the province in which the franchised location is situated. This is because a court order under Hawaiian or other US law may well have no application in Canada and the franchisor may be forced to have its action re-heard in a Canadian court. In short, the franchisor should always select the jurisdiction in which the franchisee has assets as its governing law.

13.11 Survival of Covenants

The terms and conditions of this Agreement, which by their nature require performance by the Franchisee or others after assignment, expiration, or termination shall remain enforceable notwithstanding the assignment, expiration, or termination of this Agreement.

13.12 Interpretation and Liability

The word "Franchisee" may be applicable to one or more persons, firms, or corporations, as the case may be, and the singular shall include the plural, and the masculine shall include the feminine and neuter, and vice versa; and if there is more than one person, firm, or corporation referred to as the Franchisee hereunder, their obligations and liabilities are joint and several.

13.13 Without Limitation

The words "includes," "including," and "inclusive" and the phrases "in particular," "such as," and "for example" shall be interpreted and construed so as not to limit the generality of the words of general application or nature that precede those words.

13.14 Other Documents Included

The words "this Agreement" shall be deemed to include all other agreements and instruments in effect between the Franchisee and the Franchisor (and the Franchisor's affiliates), where the context so permits.

If there is a sublease general security agreement or another agreement as part of the "package," clause **13.14** confirms that it is all the same agreement.

13.15 No Withholding

The Franchisee agrees that it will not, on the grounds of alleged non-performance by the Franchisor of any of its obligations hereunder, or in the event of any dispute, or a claim of the Franchisee, or for any other reason whatsoever, withhold payment of any amounts due to the Franchisor. The Franchisee acknowledges that the withholding of payments by the Franchisee will cause irreparable harm to the Franchisor and to the EMMA & JEREMY'S System, by not maintaining the uniformity and integrity thereof, and by hindering the ability of the Franchisor to meet and to continue to meet its obligations to the EMMA & JEREMY'S System and to the Franchisee and its other Franchisees. For these reasons, the Franchisee agrees that in any action brought by the Franchisor to enforce payment, the balance of convenience between the parties rests with the Franchisor.

In many franchise disputes, the franchisee wrongfully withholds the payment of royalties and advertising fund monies to the franchisor. This puts the franchisor at a disadvantage by not having a revenue stream. A clause such as this creates a separate breach of the agreement that may put the franchisee in a "bad spot" should he or she withhold payment of royalties or advertising monies to the franchisor.

13.16 Not Binding Unless Signed by Franchisor

This Agreement shall only be binding as between the parties on the execution by the Franchisor.

13.17 Time of Essence

Time shall be of the essence for all purposes of this Agreement.

13.18 Notices

Any notice required or permitted to be given under this Agreement shall be in writing and shall be deemed to have been duly given if delivered by hand or sent by fax to the Franchisor and the Guarantor (if such notice is required to be given to the Guarantor) at their respective addresses as shown on the first page of this Agreement; and to the Franchisee at the address shown on the first page of this Agreement or at the Franchised Location address (if the Franchisee is still in the possession or control of the Franchised Business at the Franchised Location at the time); or to such other address or fax number as the respective parties may in writing advise. Any such notice shall be deemed to have been given and received, if delivered when delivered; if sent by fax, on the same business day as the sending thereof.

The notices in my agreements are sent by courier and not by mail, as mail is too unreliable. (Email is somewhat unreliable.) Fax is sometimes used for the purposes of giving notice, but if so, each party's fax number should be provided in the agreement. Believe it or not, one still sees agreements where notices can be provided by telex!

13.19 Enurement

This Agreement shall enure to the benefit of and be binding upon the parties hereto and their respective heirs, estates, executors, administrators, legal personal representatives, successors, and permitted assigns.

13.20 Submission of Agreement

The submission of this Agreement to the Franchisee does not constitute an offer, and this Agreement shall become effective only upon execution by both the Franchisor and the Franchisee.

13.21 Risk

Although it is the Franchisor's hope and expectation that the franchise relationship between the parties will be successful, all business ventures, especially in the highly competitive food services business have risks, and there are risks involved in owning and operating an EMMA & JEREMY'S franchise, and in becoming an EMMA & JEREMY'S Internet Café & Donut Emporium franchisee. Accordingly, the Franchisee acknowledges to the Franchisor that the Franchisee is fully aware of those risks, and that the decision to apply to us to become an EMMA & JEREMY'S Internet Café & Donut Emporium franchisee, and the subsequent decision by the Franchisee to execute this Franchise Agreement and the other agreements referred to herein or contemplated hereby was the Franchisee's, after a thorough and comprehensive investigation by the Franchisee, and with the assistance of legal and financial advisors of the Franchisee's choosing. The Franchisee confirms that it has not received or relied upon any guarantees, express or implied, as to the revenues, sales, profits, working capital requirements, break-even point, or potential success of the EMMA & JEREMY'S Internet Café & Donut Emporium franchisee contemplated by this Agreement or any other matter that is not expressly contained or referred to in this Agreement or its schedules. The Franchisee further acknowledges that any information obtained in the course of the Franchisee's due diligence from other EMMA & JEREMY'S Internet Café & Donut Emporium franchisees, relating to sales, profits, or otherwise does not constitute information obtained from the Franchisor, or from its Affiliates and that the Franchisor makes no representation as to the accuracy of any such information. The Franchisee further acknowledges that it has not received or relied on any representations about the franchise made by the Franchisor, its Affiliates, or its officers, directors, employees, or agents that are not contained in this Agreement, its schedules, or the other agreements referred to in or contemplated by this Agreement, and that this Franchise Agreement supersedes all oral or written understandings, negotiations, discussions, and agreements respecting the business relationship between us as covered by this Agreement.

This provision reconfirms the fact that you have done your due diligence on the franchisor, there are no representations of success, and that you acknowledge that there are risks and that the business may not be successful. This sort of language is repeated in a number of places within the franchise agreement, all to the same end. That is, you entered the agreement without any undue pressure or misrepresentations by the franchisor. This is because the vast majority of legal actions against franchisors alleged that the franchisor had made a misrepresentation in the sales process.

13.22 No Inconsistency

The Franchisee also acknowledges and agrees that the Franchisor is relying on the Franchisee to bring forward in writing, at the time this Agreement is executed by the Franchisee, any matters inconsistent with the acknowledgements made by the Franchisee and contained in this Agreement, and in particular, this Article 13. The Franchisee agrees that if any of the statements or matters described in Article 13 (or otherwise) are not true, correct, and complete, then the Franchisee will make a handwritten statement next to its signature on the execution page of this Agreement so that the Franchisor may address and resolve any issue(s) at the time of such execution.

If you see this provision, and there is a conflict between what you are told and what you are signing, you are to make a note of it at the end of the document. Otherwise, it is presumed there is no inconsistency in the terms of the agreement, particularly the provision that there have been no representations or warrantees other than what is contained in the document.

As a lawyer for franchisors and franchisees, I like this clause. It gives the franchisee a chance of stating what representations were made, if any. In any litigation for misrepresentation, the franchisor can say, "You had the chance to comment about this when you signed the agreement and you did not."

13.23 Definitions

In this Agreement, the following words and expressions have the following meanings:

(a) "Affiliate" means any person or entity that controls, is controlled by, or is under common control with another person or entity. As to the Franchisee, it means any owner of any interest in your Franchisee, any employee or agent of your Franchised Business, and/or any independent contractor performing functions for, or on behalf, of your Franchised Business, and any entity controlled by any of the foregoing.

(b) "Agreement" means this Franchise Agreement and all schedules, instruments attached or supplemental to this Agreement.

(c) "Brand" means the EMMA & JEREMY'S Internet Café & Donut Emporium brand, as applied to various goods and/or services as authorized by us.

(d) "Confidential Information" includes all information relating to the operation of an EMMA & JEREMY'S Internet Café & Donut Emporium or the System, including all current and future:

    i) Manuals, training, techniques, processes, policies, procedures, systems, data, and know how regarding the development, marketing, operation, and franchising of an EMMA & JEREMY'S Internet Café & Donut Emporium;

ii)   specifications and information about Products and Services; and

iii)   all information regarding customers and suppliers, including any statistical and/or financial information and all customer and other lists. Specifically, the Franchisor owns and controls all domain names and URLs relating to any and all EMMA & JEREMY'S Internet Café & Donut Emporium locations, as well as all information, lists, and data related to past, present, and future customers of the Franchisee's EMMA & JEREMY'S Internet Café & Donut Emporium. The Franchisee's only interest in any of this Confidential Information is the right to use such information pursuant to this Agreement.

(e)   "Designated Equipment" means equipment that meets the Franchisor's requirements and that the Franchisee must obtain and use in the operation of the EMMA & JEREMY'S Internet Café & Donut Emporium location.

(f)   "Designated Services" means services that meet the Franchisor's requirements and that the Franchisee must use in the operation of its EMMA & JEREMY'S Internet Café & Donut Emporium location.

(g)   "Designated Products" means products or services that the Franchisee must purchase and sell in the operation of its EMMA & JEREMY'S Internet Café & Donut Emporium location.

(h)   "Franchised Business" or "Franchised EMMA & JEREMY'S Internet Café & Donut Emporium Business" means the EMMA & JEREMY'S Internet Café & Donut Emporium business the Franchisee owns and operates from the Franchised Location Premises in accordance with the EMMA & JEREMY'S System, the Manuals, the Standards, and the Trade-marks.

(i)   "Franchise" means the right to operate an EMMA & JEREMY'S Internet Café & Donut Emporium at the Franchised Location Premises under the terms of this Agreement.

(j)   "Intellectual Property" means, regardless of the form or medium involved —

(i)   all EMMA & JEREMY'S Internet Café & Donut Emporium software, including the data and information processed or stored;

(ii)   the Operations Manuals and all other directives, policies, or information the Franchisor uses from time to time;

(iii)   all customer relationships and information;

(iv)   the Trade-marks;

(v) all Confidential Information and trade secrets; and

(vi) all other proprietary, copyrightable, and/or trade secret information and materials developed, acquired, licensed, or used by the Franchisor in our operation of the System.

(k) "Similar Business" means any enterprise that offers, is otherwise involved in, or deals with any goods, products, and/or services similar to those offered from EMMA & JEREMY'S Internet Café & Donut Emporium locations.

(l) "Products" and "Services" means goods, products, and services designated by us for use, sale, or otherwise to be provided to and used at or sold from the Franchisee's EMMA & JEREMY'S Internet Café & Donut Emporium location.

(m) "Initial Franchise Fee" has the meaning set forth in Section 4.1 of this Agreement.

(n) "Location" or "Premises" or "Franchised Location" or "Franchised Premises" or "Franchised Location Premises" means the premises for the operation of the franchised EMMA & JEREMY'S Internet Café & Donut Emporium business as specified in Schedule "A."

(o) "Advertising Fund" means the fund established and administered pursuant to Article 5 of this Agreement.

(p) "Operations Manuals" or "Manuals" mean collectively, all operations manuals or other manuals and all books, pamphlets, memoranda, directives, instructions, videos, CD-ROMs, and other materials prepared by or on behalf of the franchisor (whether in written, machine readable, Internet accessible, or any other form), setting out the methods, procedures, techniques, standards, and specifications of the EMMA & JEREMY'S Internet Café & Donut Emporium system, as may be modified or amended from time to time by the Franchisor.

(q) "Royalty" or "Royalties" or "Continuing Royalties" has the meaning set forth in section 4.2 of this Agreement.

(r) "Standards" or "EMMA & JEREMY'S Internet Café & Donut Emporium Standards" means those standards of operation set forth by the Franchisor from time to time in the Manuals or otherwise specifying the details of the EMMA & JEREMY'S System that are required to be complied with by all franchised EMMA & JEREMY'S Internet Café & Donut Emporium outlets in Canada.

(s) "System" or the "EMMA & JEREMY'S System" means the distinctive system and business format for the development, establishment, and operation of EMMA &

JEREMY'S Internet Café & Donut Emporium, which business is distinguished by certain proprietary knowledge, procedures, formats, systems, forms, printed materials, applications, specifications, standards, and techniques authorized by the Franchisor and all identified through trade names and trade-marks owned by the Franchisor as may be added to, changed, modified, or otherwise revised from time to time.

(t)   "National Accounts" means classes of special customers (which may include national accounts, other large businesses, government agencies, or otherwise) designated by us from time to time in our discretion.

(u)   "Trade Dress" means the EMMA & JEREMY'S store design and image authorized by the Franchisor and subject to change by the Franchisor in its sole discretion.

(v)   "Term" means the term of this Agreement as specified in section 3.1 as may be renewed in accordance with section 3.2.

(w)   "Trade-marks" or "Marks" means the trade-marks, Trade Dress, designs, graphics, logos, and other commercial symbols now and in the future owned by the Franchisor to which the Franchisor may designate from time to time for use in connection with the Franchised Business to identify the services and/or products offered by EMMA & JEREMY'S Internet Café & Donut Emporium outlets.

Sometimes, the agreement will define certain important terms that occur from time to time in the document. This may be provided at the beginning or at the end of the agreement (although it's normally in the beginning). Defined terms are normally in capital letters throughout the agreement, so when you see something in capitals, chances are, it has a specific meaning, and it's defined somewhere. Definitions are important and should be carefully reviewed, especially matters such as gross sales.

13.24 No Reliance by the Franchisee

The franchisee acknowledges that the success of the franchised business is dependent upon the personal efforts of the franchisee, or the franchisee's partners or officers if the franchisee is a partnership or corporation. The franchisee acknowledges that neither the franchisor nor any other party has guaranteed to the franchisee or warranted that the franchisee will succeed in the operation of the franchised business whether express, implied, purported, or alleged, in entering into this agreement. The franchisee acknowledges that any financial information that may have been provided to it by the franchisor or any other party acting on behalf of the franchisor was provided for information or guidance purposes only, to assist the franchisee in making its own financial forecasts or projections, and that neither the franchisor nor any other party has given any warranty of accuracy or reliability to the franchisee in connection therewith. The franchisor shall not be liable to the franchisee in any way

for any losses sustained by the franchisee in the operation of the franchised business, it being understood and agreed that the franchisee is an independent contractor entitled to retain all profits derived from its operations of the franchised business after payment of all sums due to the franchisor and others.

These sorts of provisions are usually written in capital letters or in bold immediately before the signature provisions. It effectively states that the franchisee or the principal of the franchisee has not relied upon any representation or warranty of the franchisor in entering into the agreement.

Most legal proceedings commenced by franchisees against franchisors are for misrepresentation. That is the franchisor, or its agents, are alleged to have misrepresented certain features of the franchised business in order to induce the franchisee into entering into the contract. "They said I would make $100,000 a year as profit," or "They said I could buy supplies at market price," and so on. This provision is a repetition of other provisions in the agreement but is normal in Canadian franchise agreements. It allows the franchisor to point to this part of the agreement and indicate that there could be no representation other than what was contained in the agreement because the franchisee read the bold print.

IN WITNESS WHEREOF, the Franchisor and the Franchisee have caused this Agreement to be executed as of the day and year first written below.

FRANCHISOR:

EMMA & JEREMY'S INTERNET CAFÉ & DONUT EMPORIUM LTD.

Per:

_____ DATE: _____

(Signature)   *(Title)*

I acknowledge that prior to the date that I have executed this agreement, or have paid any consideration therefor, I received, read, and understood a complete copy of this agreement with all terms and conditions inserted, and I further acknowledge that prior to the date that I have executed this agreement, or have paid any consideration therefor to franchisor, I have had adequate opportunity to review this agreement with legal counsel and other advisors of my own choosing and that I am aware of the terms and conditions of this agreement and of the business risks involved in entering into this agreement and the business contemplated hereby.

The undersigned guarantor(s) each agree that in consideration of the premises and of the granting of this franchise agreement to franchisee at the separate request of each of us individually, all of the undersigned guarantors (if more than one) are personally bound individually, unconditionally, irrevocably, jointly, and severally with franchisee to observe and perform all of the terms and conditions of this agreement. All of the undersigned hereby waive all benefits of division, discussion, notice, and disclosure and agree that no dealings of franchisor with franchisee or any other party shall discharge or reduce the continuing obligations of any of the undersigned hereunder, and that in the enforcement of any of its rights, the franchisor may proceed against any of us as if the undersigned or any of us were the party primarily obligated under this agreement. The undersigned also each agree that all of the undersigned are personally so bound by those provisions of this agreement that specifically express themselves as being binding upon us personally.

FRANCHISEE:

_____

(Print name of the Franchisee Corporation)

Per:

_____   DATE:_____

*(Authorized Signatory for the Franchisee
  Corporation)*

FRANCHISEE: *(only if individual)*

_____

(Signature)

_____   DATE:_____

(Authorized Signatory for the Franchisee)

GUARANTORS:
SIGNED, SEALED, AND DELIVERED by   )
_____   )
(Print name of Guarantor here)   )
)
_____   )
(Name of Witness)   )
)

_____)
(Address of Witness)   )   _____
)   *(Signature of Guarantor) (Seal)*
)
_____)
(Occupation of Witness)   )

DATE:_____

SIGNED, SEALED, AND DELIVERED by   )
)
_____)
(Print name of Guarantor here)   )
)
_____)
(Name of Witness)   )
)
_____)   _____
(Address of Witness)   )   *(Signature of Guarantor) (Seal)*
)
_____)
(Occupation of Witness)   )

DATE:_____

SAMPLE 2
SCHEDULE A

SCHEDULE "A"
SPECIFIC TERMS

1. The address of the Franchised Location Premises is as follows:
673 Dundas St., London, Ontario

2. The Franchised Territory is as follows:

   (See drawing attached, if applicable)

   2 km radius around the franchised location premises.

3. The following person(s) are "owner-operators" and shall participate actively on a full-time basis in the management and operation of the Franchised Business and are bound by the covenants contained in this Agreement including but without limitation, the covenants contained in Article 6.

   Geoffrey Bickerstakk

4. The effective date of this Agreement is <u>October 1, 2005</u> with opening <u>January 15, 2006</u>.

5. The term of this Agreement is <u>5</u> years, commencing as of <u>October 1, 2005</u> and ending <u>September 30, 2010</u>.

6. The Initial Franchise Fee is $ <u>30,000</u>.

7. The amount of Continuing Royalties is <u>6% of gross sales</u>.

8. Local Advertising Obligation is <u>2% of gross sales</u>.

9. Opening promotion is $ <u>2,500</u>.

10. Documentation Fee is $ <u>1,000</u>.

11. Assignment Fee is $ <u>10% of initial franchise fee</u>.

12. Special conditions re: renewal *(if applicable)*

13. Additional Terms of Turnkey Development

(See attached list, if applicable)

14.   List of Equipment

(See attached list, if applicable)

INITIALS: Franchisor:_____

Franchisee:_____

PRINCIPALS AND OWNERSHIP OF FRANCHISEE

The names of the shareholders or partners and their voting and equity interests in the Franchisee are as follows:

Names Of Shareholders Or Partners	% Voting Interest	% Equity Interest
Geoffrey Bickerstakk	50	50
Niel Davies	50	50

The directors and officers of the Franchisee are as follows:

NAMES OF DIRECTORS:

Geoffrey Bickerstakk, President

Niel Davies, Vice President

INITIALS:

Franchisor:_____

Franchisee:_____

PART 3

THE DISCLOSURE DOCUMENT

15
DISCLOSURE IN CANADA

1. ONTARIO AND ALBERTA DISCLOSURE DOCUMENTS

As of 2004, Alberta and Ontario were the only Canadian jurisdictions that had legislation specifically regulating franchisors and the sale of franchises. PEI adopted legislation in 2007. New Brunswick has enacted legislation as of 2009, but regulations have not yet come into force. Other provinces are considering legislation. Alberta was the first Canadian jurisdiction to enact franchise legislation, having enacted its own franchise laws in the early 1970s. The original Alberta legislation was modelled on the franchise laws of California and required the franchisor to "register" in that province in much the same way as franchisors must register in California, Hawaii, Illinois, Indiana, Maryland, Michigan, Minnesota, New York, North Dakota, Oregon, Rhode Island, South Dakota, Virginia, Washington, and Wisconsin. I propose to only discuss the Alberta and Ontario laws.

1.1 Alberta

New legislation was enacted in Alberta in 1995 replacing the previous regulatory regime with a "disclosure only" regime. This means that franchisors no longer have to file a "prospectus" (similar to a US FDD) with the Alberta Securities Commission, and spend endless hours negotiating the completeness and accuracy of the prospectus, or the terms and conditions under which the franchisor will be allowed to sell franchises in Alberta with that commission. Sadly, for lawyers, these legislative changes also reduced legal fees that arose from all this complicated, time consuming, and generally lucrative compliance work!

The legislative changes of 1995 obliged franchisors selling franchises in Alberta to provide a disclosure document to all prospective franchisees. This document must contain a disclosure of all material facts relating to the franchise and the franchisor — full, plain, and true disclosure that would allow a prospective franchisee to make an informed decision as to whether he or she should make the investment and acquire the franchise.

Now there is no involvement by any provincial regulatory body. There is no vetting or administrative review by the Alberta Securities Commission. Franchisors who fail to do the following are liable under the statute:

- Provide a disclosure document to a prospective franchisee as required under the act

- Disclose all material facts (including those matters listed in the legislation)

- Provide prospective franchisees with a requisite period of time between the date the disclosure document is delivered to the franchisee and the date the franchise and related agreements are executed (i.e., 14 days)

The courts will assess the remedy for non-compliance, which can be significant and involve damages against the franchisor or recession of the contract (i.e., putting the franchisee in the same financial position he or she would have been in had he or she not entered the franchise).

1.2 Ontario

Similar (but by no means identical) legislation came into effect in Ontario in early 2001. This legislation is called the *Arthur Wishart Act* (Franchise Disclosure), 2000.

What is interesting is that more and more prospective franchisees in the non-regulated provinces (i.e., British Columbia, Saskatchewan, Manitoba, and Quebec) are being provided with Ontario/Alberta disclosure documents, even though the laws of their particular province don't require it. In some ways, Ontario and Alberta are making their franchise laws the laws for the rest of Canada. This may benefit prospective franchisees in the other provinces, as this arguably means the disclosure documents given to them are pre-contractual inducements and warrantees.

An Ontario or Alberta disclosure document is required to be delivered to a prospective franchisee at least 14 days before signing any franchise agreements or paying any money to the franchisor. In Ontario, no franchise agreement can be entered prior to disclosure having been made and the requisite time period having passed. A deposit agreement will be deemed to be a franchise agreement under that statute. In Alberta, fully refundable deposits may be taken prior to disclosure by the franchisor, but only in an amount not greater than 20 percent of the franchisor's initial franchise fee and only where any deposit agreement is limited to dealing with the deposit, the location or territory, and confidentiality and non-use of the franchisor's information and materials.

Under the laws of both provinces, the franchisor is required to disclose all material facts relating to the franchised business and the franchisor's history, but no government regulatory approval is required respecting the disclosure document or the franchise agreement; somewhat analogous to the US FTC Rule. These disclosure documents are not on the public record, and are usually only available from the franchisor or its sales agents.

2. WHAT MUST GO IN A DISCLOSURE DOCUMENT?

In Alberta and Ontario, certain matters are required by law to be disclosed. Those matters are essentially (but not exclusively) as follows:

- Information concerning the franchisor and its business background

- Previous criminal convictions and pending criminal charges against the franchisor and its directors and officers

- Civil litigation and liabilities of the franchisor and its directors, officers, and associates. (Are they being sued? Is there a judgment against any of them?)

- Administrative proceedings and orders. (Is there a government order issued against the franchisor or its directors, officers, and associates or otherwise affecting the franchised business?)

- Bankruptcy. (Has the franchisor or any of its directors, officers, and associates been bankrupt over the past six years?)

- Nature of the business. (What is the franchised system that you are acquiring? How, in general terms, does it work?)

- Initial franchise fees and other fees. The disclosure document must list all fees you are required to pay (e.g., renewal fees, royalties, training fees, assignment fees, interest, etc.).

- Other fees and expenses. (Perhaps there is legislation requiring bonding or training or other qualifications set by provincial law, such as with direct sellers or travel agents, etc. For example, if a legal franchise was offered, disclosure would have to be made of the requirement to be a lawyer and of the need to pay practice fees and insurance.)

- Initial investment required

- Financing provided by the franchisor. (If any is being provided.)

- Working capital requirements. (If any.)

- Restrictions on sources of products and services from whom you can buy

- Restrictions on what products and services you may sell

- Rebates and other benefits flowing to the franchisor. (If so, what are they?)

- Obligations to participate in the actual operation of the franchised business. (Are owner operators required or can you hire full-time managers?)

- Special licenses required to run the business (e.g., legal and accounting franchise firms have special licenses, as do travel agencies in some provinces)

- List of all existing franchisee and franchisor outlets, with contact information

- List of all franchise closures

- If earnings claims are made, there must be specific disclosure as to how the claim was arrived at and how the assumptions were made.

- Summary of the provisions dealing with termination, renewal, and assignment of the franchise

- Disclosure as to whether the franchisor allows disputes to be mediated

- Franchisor's policy on granting territories

- Financial statements must be attached

- In Alberta, the document must contain provisions directly from the statute respecting rescission and effect of cancellation as well as your right of action for damages

- In Ontario, there are other requirements whereby the document must contain certain mandated notices (e.g., credit history notice, mediation notice)

- Alberta and Ontario law also impose upon both parties a statutory duty to act fairly and in good faith in the performance of the franchise agreement.

3. WHAT HAPPENS IF THE FRANCHISE AGREEMENT IS CALLED A LICENSE AGREEMENT?

As you read in Chapter 1, franchises are essentially licenses. This is important to note in circumstances in which the Ontario and Alberta disclosure laws come into play. The so-called licensor may call its business system a licence, and explain to you, "It's a licence, not a franchise so the Ontario and Alberta laws don't apply." Wrong! If the business system meets the definition of a franchise as set out in the two statutes (depending, of course, on which province the franchise relates to as the acts are different), it's a franchise, regardless of what the franchisor calls it. In short, if it walks like a duck and quacks like a duck, it's likely not a horse, even though it's kept in a stable! Your franchise lawyer will be able to assist you in assessing whether or not it is a duck!

Be aware that business arrangements that are characterized as distributorships or other business opportunities may also be franchises under the Ontario or Alberta laws. If the business opportunity you are examining proves not to be a franchise, it may still be a business regulated by other provincial and federal laws, such as the multilevel marketing provisions of the *Competition Act* and the respective consumer protection, direct sellers, and trade practices acts in force in those provinces that have such laws. They may prescribe "cooling off periods" and a form of prescribed disclosure as well, although not to the level prescribed by the Ontario and Alberta franchise laws.

16

ALBERTA AND ONTARIO DISCLOSURE DOCUMENT

This chapter includes an expedited sample disclosure document for both Ontario and Alberta. Please note it is not a full version of an Alberta/Ontario disclosure document, as disclosure documents tend to be very long and detailed, containing tables, financial statements, warnings, and certain provisions mandated by statute. Rather than including all the information that would normally be required in such a document, this summary version includes highlights and commentary on the sorts of things that you might wish to investigate further, or which should be cause for concern. As with the franchise agreement noted in Part 2, there are deliberate errors, omissions, and embellishments in the disclosure document to alert you to some important information.

EMMA & JEREMY'S INTERNET CAFÉ & DONUT EMPORIUM FRANCHISE DISCLOSURE DOCUMENT

Pursuant to the requirements of Ontario and Alberta

Now that both Ontario and Alberta have franchise legislation requiring a comprehensive disclosure document to be delivered to prospective franchisees well prior to the franchisor entering into a franchise with the franchisee, some (but not all) Canadian lawyers have created "joint disclosure documents" that are meant to satisfy the requirements of both jurisdictions in one document rather than having to prepare two documents (i.e., one for Alberta and one for Ontario). Not all lawyers prepare joint documents, so you may find the franchisor has one document that satisfies Ontario's requirements and one that satisfies Alberta's. Although there are some significant differences in the disclosure requirements under each province's laws, a joint disclosure document will indicate that certain provisions are applicable to Alberta franchisees and certain provisions are applicable to Ontario franchisees.

EMMA & JEREMY'S INTERNET CAFÉ & DONUT EMPORIUM LTD.

(A British Columbia Company)

of 1121 Woodburn Avenue, Vancouver, British Columbia

ONTARIO WARNING

A Disclosure Document must be given to the prospective buyer of a franchise (the "Franchisee") at least 14 days before the prospective Franchisee signs **any** agreement relating to the Franchise, or the payment of **any** consideration by the prospective Franchisee relating to the Franchise. This Disclosure Document only summarizes certain important aspects of the Franchise Agreement. The Franchise Agreement is the document that will legally bind the Franchisor and the Franchisee, which accordingly should be carefully studied in detail. It is attached as Schedule "A."

This warning is an example of a statutory requirement under Ontario law. The warning is not required under Alberta law, but in a joint document the warning will be there anyway. Note that in Ontario, no money can be exchanged and no document can be signed relating to the franchise for a period of 14 days from the date the document is delivered to the franchisee. (Note: Delivery cannot be made by email or fax under Ontario law.)

The *Arthur Wishart Act* (Franchise Disclosure) of Ontario also requires that the following information be provided at the beginning of this Disclosure Document:

This warning is also an example of a statutory requirement under Ontario law. The warning is not required under Alberta law, although it's good advice in any event. Alberta has chosen to require franchisors to reproduce certain sections of its act dealing with remedies.

A commercial credit report is a report that may include information on the franchisor's business background, banking information, credit history, and trade references. Such reports may be obtained from private credit reporting companies and may provide information useful in making an investment decision.

Independent legal and financial advice in relation to the franchise agreement should be sought prior to entering into the franchise agreement.

A prospective franchisee is strongly encouraged to contact any current or previous franchisees prior to entering into the franchise agreement.

> **The cost of goods and services acquired under the franchise agreement may not correspond to the lowest cost of the goods and services available in the marketplace.**

1. FRANCHISOR INFORMATION/BUSINESS BACKGROUND

(a)   The name and principal business address of the Franchisor:

Emma & Jeremy's Internet Café & Donut Emporium Ltd.

> You or your lawyer can check to see if this company is incorporated by performing a corporation search with your province's corporations branch. You would normally have your lawyer do this online (or you or your lawyer would retain agents to do this). You might also have your lawyer do a search of the Personal Property Security Registry (or comparative registry) to see what financing statements or other borrowings are recorded against the franchisor and its assets.

As of the date of this Disclosure Document, the Franchisor utilizes its business address at 1121 Woodburn Avenue, Vancouver, British Columbia, V7E 4R2.

The Franchisor also expects to use from time to time its registered offices of SULLIVAN, LONG, & DEPHIPPIPI, at Suite 368 – 850 Blanshard Street, Victoria, British Columbia. The Franchisor expects to also be operating from an Ontario office and Alberta office when such offices have been formally established.

> A franchisor is required to state its business address but may also indicate its registered offices, which will be its lawyer's office in most cases. (**Note:** This particular law firm is a totally fictitious creation, as are all other law firms and individuals noted herein.)

(b)   The names under which the Franchisor does or intends to do business:

The Franchisor will do business under the trade name and trade-mark "EMMA & JEREMY'S INTERNET CAFÉ & DONUT EMPORIUM," which it has the licensed right to use from its licensor, EMMA & JEREMY'S INTERNET CAFÉ & DONUT EMPORIUM INTERNATIONAL LIMITED, a Delaware Company, being the worldwide owner of the Emma & Jeremy's Internet Café & Donut Emporium System and the licensor of the Franchisor under this Agreement (such company and its affiliates and subsidiaries are hereinafter collectively called the "Licensor"). The Canadian trade-mark particulars are as follows, and as the date of this Disclosure Document, such mark has not yet matured to registration:

> If, for whatever reason, the trade-marks are held in the name of a different company (or person) than the franchisor, you should make further inquiries, as the

trade-marks may have been licensed to the franchisor and the franchisor's rights depend on the license being in compliance. The point here is that you should investigate who the trade-mark owner is, and how the franchisor acquired its rights.

Application #421575 "EMMA & JEREMY'S INTERNET CAFÉ & DONUT EMPORIUM" (and design).

As it was mentioned in Chapter 10, it may be useful to investigate particulars as to trade-mark registration and status (i.e., registration number and ownership).

Applicant: Pat Nutella

Wares and Services:

Wares (1) Donuts, coffee, muffins, cookies, sushi, shoes, computers, edible sunscreen

Services (1) Operating a Café with a dedicated Internet connection for customers to plug in their laptops or otherwise connect wirelessly; serving coffee, cookies, donuts, muffins, sushi, shoes, and edible sunscreen; use of computers; providing weight-loss counselling. The Franchising of outlets selling such items and providing such services.

Although, thankfully, you will never see a donut and Internet café business that sells sushi, shoes, and provides weight-loss counselling, the point here is for you to critically examine the franchised business and assess whether you think there is a future in such a business or whether it is a flash in the proverbial pan.

The said application specifies that the Canadian trade-mark was filed on June 28, 2004, with the Canadian Trade-Marks Office (Canadian Intellectual Property Office) on a proposed use basis.

As the mark has been applied for and has not yet matured to registration, the Franchisor cannot guarantee that the mark will be registered, although, based on assurances from its Licensor, it expects the mark to mature to registration in due course.

Note this trade-mark is not formally registered. It appears from this disclosure document that an application has been filed for the mark with the Canadian Intellectual Property Office, but registration of the mark has not yet been secured.

The trade-mark process can take anywhere between one and three years. What happens if you have acquired the franchise and commenced using these trade-marks, only to find that the franchisor cannot obtain a registration of the trade-mark? Will you be required by the franchisor to choose other trade-marks and to spend the money required to "re-identify" with another brand?

Note as well the applicant for the mark is not the franchisor under this disclosure document. So who really owns or controls it if it is not the franchisor?

If the franchisor does not have the right to use the trade-mark, perhaps another entity might have the right to stop you from using the mark. So it's important to assess the status of the mark, especially if it is not yet registered, and even more so if some party other than the franchisor is noted as the applicant. Your franchise lawyer should be able to help you with this.

(c)   The principal business address of the Franchisor and the name and address of the persons authorized to accept service in the Provinces of Alberta and Ontario:

Sometimes the franchisor will not have established an office in Alberta or Ontario before franchising. It is not uncommon for the franchisor to use its lawyer's offices.

Principal Business Address in Alberta:

As the Franchisor is newly established, no formal office is set up in the Province of Alberta or Ontario as of the date of this Disclosure Document. It is anticipated that the Franchisor will utilize its British Columbia offices until such time the Alberta and Ontario offices are established.

Persons authorized to accept service in Alberta on Franchisor's behalf:

CHARNEY, TODESCO, & THOMPSON

424 Bickerstaff Place, Edmonton, Alberta, T7J 3P6

Attention: BALTHZAR E. TODESCO

Principal business address in Ontario:

Persons authorized to accept service in Ontario on the Franchisee's behalf:

PATTON, APPS, LEERING, MCNAIR, & CORRIGAN

44 St. Komenda Avenue East, Suite 800, Toronto, Ontario, M4T 2S3

Attention: JOHN STUART DONEGAN

(d)   The business form of the Franchisor:

The Franchisor is a corporation incorporated under the laws of British Columbia on February 5, 2003, under No. D-2459.

As of the date of this Disclosure Document the Franchisor has no affiliated companies that are involved in its franchising activities; however, the principal of the Franchisor (Horace Allabarton or his wife Pat Nutella) owns or will own 100% of the issued and outstanding shares of **D-2459 (2004) BC** Ltd., which company has been incorporated for the purpose of owning and operating certain individual franchised outlets.

EMMA & JEREMY'S INTERNET CAFÉ & DONUT EMPORIUM LTD. (being the Franchisor herein) is to be owned by Elodie N. Roddy (or a corporation owned directly or indirectly by her) as to 33%; **127474 Ontario Ltd.** (being a company owned directly or indirectly by the principal the Franchisor, Horace Allabarton or his wife Pat Nutella) as to 41%; and 34676 Yukon Ltd. (being a company directly or indirectly owned by Coleman Chung) as to 10%. Coleman Chung is a resident of Delaware, USA. Horace Allabarton is a resident of Burnaby, BC. Elodie N. Roddy is a resident of Oak Bay, BC. All the above companies have registered offices at Suite 368 – 850 Blanshard Street, Victoria, British Columbia. As the Franchisor is newly incorporated, the share structure, although agreed as between the parties, is not fully documented, and it is expected that Ms. Nutella will have her or her corporation's shares issued shortly.

This convoluted and almost incomprehensible description of ownership should persuade you that the ownership of the franchisor and its right to franchise is convoluted and incomprehensible. Being convoluted doesn't necessarily mean that something is untoward or suspicious. It just means that you have to examine the ownership more carefully, chart the ownership out like a map and probably have a few words with a franchise lawyer about it.

There would appear to be many different rights holders in the franchisor under this disclosure document and the franchisor appears to have been granted the rights to franchise in Canada by a US company. If the US company granted rights to all of Canada, did the US company comply with Ontario law and provide the franchisor with an Ontario disclosure document? If so, that would be a useful document to review (if the franchisor allowed you to review it). If the grant to the Canadian franchisor included Ontario, why wouldn't the US franchisor have made such disclosure?

The EMMA & JEREMY'S INTERNET CAFÉ & DONUT EMPORIUM franchise concept is new to Canada, and as of the date of this Disclosure Document there are 3 franchised stores in operation. As of the date of this Disclosure Document, there are no operational stores in either Alberta or Ontario, although the Franchisor has entered into a number of deposit agreements with interested parties.

If deposit agreements have been entered in Ontario before the requisite 14-day waiting period, the *Wishart Act* has been breached and the franchisor is in some legal trouble.

(e)   The length of time the Franchisor has conducted a business of the type to be operated by the Franchisee:

The Franchisor commenced business in approximately October, 2003. It acquired the Master Franchise rights for all of Canada (including the Provinces of Ontario and Alberta) from EMMA & JEREMY'S INTERNET CAFÉ & DONUT EMPORIUM INTERNATIONAL LIMITED as of December 22, 2003. Accordingly, the Franchisor has only recently commenced its franchising operations of the EMMA & JEREMY'S INTERNET CAFÉ & DONUT EMPORIUM system and business concept in Canada.

Neither the Franchisor, nor its principal, Horace Allabarton, have offered franchises in Canada in any business other than with respect to the EMMA & JEREMY'S INTERNET CAFÉ & DONUT EMPORIUM business referred to in the Franchisor's form of Franchise Agreement and as otherwise disclosed herein.

The disclosure document is required to contain certain information mandated by statue, but it is also, to some extent, a marketing document. The franchisor gets to tell a prospective purchaser all about the franchise it is "selling." All material facts have to be disclosed, and each of the Alberta and Ontario statues defines what a material fact is. (Think of it as any fact that if known to the franchisee would have affected the franchisee's decision to buy the franchise in the first place.)

It is imperative for the franchisor to disclose all material facts relating to the franchise even if they are unhelpful, prejudicial, and on the whole, bad. The franchisor gets the opportunity to put these unfortunate material facts (if there are any) in the best possible light. Sometimes unhelpful, prejudicial, and bad material facts can be spun in such a way through the use of ingenuous legal and marketing language to soften the effect. A sow's ear can be a silk purse, depending upon the marketing language used. So remember that bad facts, if disclosed, will be spun to the franchisor's benefit.

In this extremely fictional example, you will see that none of the principals have particularly good qualifications to run a franchised business, let alone any other kind of business. Their backgrounds are checkered with many odd business ventures and little or no franchise experience. It is up to you to be able to cut your way through the legalese and marketing language, and assess for yourself whether you have enough information on these people and the franchise to make an informed decision. Are they the people you want to have a long-term business relationship with? Do these people have the requisite experience to successfully franchise the business, or in the fictional case below, are they just doing this because they have nothing else to do?

(f)   Names of the directors, general partners, and officers of the Franchisor who will
        have management responsibilities relating to the franchise. State each person's
        principal occupation and employers during the 5 years preceding the date of the
        Disclosure Document, as well as each person's business background:

The directors and officers of the Franchisor corporation (EMMA & JEREMY'S INTERNET
CAFÉ & DONUT EMPORIUM LTD.) are as follows:

Horace Allabarton: Chief Executive Officer/President

For the five years preceding this Disclosure Document, Mr. Allabarton has been involved
in the following activities and businesses: From January 1999 to September 1999, he was
the President of Bulashkistan (a Republic of the former USSR), which his family re-inher-
ited after the collapse of the Soviet Union in 1991 and which was forced to rejoin Russia in
2004 after the Republic was pledged as security in a game of Risk (which he subsequently
lost). He owned and managed the world's largest producer of edible sunscreen in Bulgaria.
He acquired 2 Foxtrot-Class submarines from the former Soviet Navy and attempted to
display them as a tourist attraction in Cuba.

Since October 2003, he has devoted his full time and efforts to bring the Emma & Jeremy's Internet Café & Donut Emporium concept to Canada.

Coleman Chung: Secretary

Coleman Chung is the secretary of the Franchisor and is to be a director of such corporation. Since October 2003, he has managed the operating Emma & Jeremy's Internet Café &
Donut Emporium business location in Vancouver, British Columbia. Prior to 2003, he was
a part-time Mustard salesman in Humboldt, Saskatchewan; head Sushi Chef at the "Food
'n Grits" Truck Stop and edible Suntan Lotion Emporium in Wala Wala, Washington; and
Senior Waiter in the Cafeteria of the BBC World Service in London.

Key Individuals:

Pat Nutella

Pat Nutella is the principal founder of Emma & Jeremy's Internet Café & Donut Emporium
and operates from worldwide headquarters in Wichita Falls, Kansas. She has diplomas in
penguin hygiene, sushi dynamics, and modern Esperanto graffitti from the University of
Mitmestimung, in Dresden, Germany. She has a diploma in advanced kayak architecture
and design from the Senewald Kinesics Institute in Banff, Alberta. She has been involved
in the Emma & Jeremy's Internet Café & Donut Emporium concept from its inception and
has been the International Company's managing director since 1997.

Again, read the biographies with a critical eye and assess whether these people have the "right stuff," or indeed the wrong stuff. Check references if you feel you should; after all, you're putting up the money.

2. PREVIOUS CONVICTIONS AND PENDING CHARGES

Franchisors must disclose whether there are any previous convictions or pending charges against the franchisor or its directors or officers or other key persons. Limitations on disclosure, such as limiting the disclosure to convictions in Canada and not disclosing the convictions or pending charges in any other jurisdiction, will not comply with the acts. So be careful of language that qualifies an item of disclosure.

3. CIVIL LITIGATION AND LIABILITIES

Franchisors must disclose whether there are any lawsuits against the franchisor or its directors or officers or other key persons. Every province has a registry (or registries) that records actions and judgments in civil court. If you have any doubts, your lawyer can check this. Often, legal actions and judgments are reported in newspapers and information regarding this might also be obtainable using an online database service or by accessing a search engine such as Google.

4. ADMINISTRATIVE PROCEEDINGS AND EXISTING ORDERS

Franchisors must disclose whether there are any administrative proceedings against the franchisor or its directors or officers or other key persons. A "cease trading order" from a securities board might be an example of this.

5. BANKRUPTCY

Franchisors must disclose whether it or its directors or officers have been bankrupt over the previous six years.

6. NATURE OF THE BUSINESS

The primary business of the Franchisor is the offer and sale of EMMA & JEREMY'S INTERNET CAFÉ & DONUT EMPORIUM Franchise businesses (the type offered here).

Franchisors always claim that they have developed a unique format and successful system. Often they have, and you recognize the brand's success. It's up to you to determine whether the system is so unique and desirable that the concept will succeed in the marketplace.

The Franchisor does not offer franchises in any other line of business, but it and its affiliates have the right to do so. The Franchisor, may, at its option, establish "corporate" EMMA & JEREMY'S INTERNET CAFÉ & DONUT EMPORIUM locations, or franchise such outlets to corporations that it or its principals have a direct or indirect interest in.

The Franchisor acquired the rights to grant EMMA & JEREMY'S INTERNET CAFÉ & DONUT EMPORIUM franchises from EMMA & JEREMY'S INTERNET CAFÉ & DONUT EMPORIUM INTERNATIONAL LIMITED, a Delaware corporation with an office located in Wala Wala, Washington, being the worldwide owner of the EMMA & JEREMY'S DONUT EMPORIUM AND INTERNET CAFÉ SYSTEM, under a separate Master Franchise Agreement entered into October 7, 2002.

The EMMA & JEREMY'S INTERNET CAFÉ & DONUT EMPORIUM business involves the sale of donuts, and potentially sushi and shoes at the Internet cafés in urban centres and use of the EMMA & JEREMY'S INTERNET CAFÉ & DONUT EMPORIUM diet donut products together with weight-loss counselling, both of which activities are carried on from the franchised location by the Franchisee and its trained staff. The Franchisor believes that weight-loss programs work best when customers can purchase donuts to respond to their need for carbohydrates. EMMA & JEREMY'S INTERNET CAFÉ & DONUT EMPORIUM INTERNATIONAL LIMITED, is a Delaware corporation with an office located at Wala Wala, Washington, USA, and is the worldwide owner of the Emma & Jeremy's Internet Café & Donut Emporium System. It was formed in Bulgaria and began offering EMMA & JEREMY'S INTERNET CAFÉ & DONUT EMPORIUM Franchises similar to this one operated in Bulgaria and the uk under the name "Edible Sunscreen and Cooking Oil Ltd." in 1994. As of the date of this Disclosure Document there are 4 Emma & Jeremy's Internet Café & Donut Emporium outlets operated corporately or franchised by Emma & Jeremy's Internet Café & Donut Emporium International or its regional franchises in Ireland, Bulgaria, Spain, and Scotland. It began offering EMMA & JEREMY'S INTERNET CAFÉ & DONUT EMPORIUM Master Franchises in approximately 2003. EMMA & JEREMY'S INTERNET CAFÉ & DONUT EMPORIUM INTERNATIONAL LIMITED will be assisting the Franchisor herein respecting matters such as training.

If the Franchisor grants the Franchisee an EMMA & JEREMY'S INTERNET CAFÉ & DONUT EMPORIUM Franchise, the Franchisee will have a contractual franchise relationship only with the Franchisor hereunder. EMMA & JEREMY'S INTERNET CAFÉ & DONUT EMPORIUM INTERNATIONAL LIMITED will not have any obligations to Franchisees, and Franchisees may look only to the Franchisor for performance under their Franchise Agreement.

The Franchisor may offer EMMA & JEREMY'S INTERNET CAFÉ & DONUT EMPORIUM Franchises in other provinces or in Ontario/Alberta on economic and/or other terms that differ from those referred to in this Disclosure Document. Also, there may be instances in which the Franchisor may be required to vary, or will vary, the terms on which a franchise is granted to suit the circumstances of a particular transaction.

There is a lot of information in the paragraph above, including the point that the franchisor may do different deals with different franchisees. How do you feel about that? The franchisor under this document has also obtained its franchise rights from another entity, meaning that its rights to franchise may be dependent on being in compliance with another agreement.

Prospective Franchisees should also understand the following business realities: A franchised EMMA & JEREMY'S INTERNET CAFÉ & DONUT EMPORIUM Business involves business risks. The Franchisor does not have the ability to reliably make any promises, estimates, representations, guarantees, or other assurances concerning the potential success any particular franchisee may have as an EMMA & JEREMY'S INTERNET CAFÉ & DONUT EMPORIUM Franchisee. The Franchisor does not guarantee the success or any level of sales volume, profits (if any), or otherwise.

During the sales process, they might well try to give you the impression that the representations made by them are accurate and you may be shown pro forma and other statements, but here, the franchisor is denying the reliability of such projections and statements if they turn out to be inaccurate. (In fairness to the franchisor, they might only prove to be inaccurate because the franchisee in question is a poor operator and not because of any flaw in the statements or other representations.)

The EMMA & JEREMY'S INTERNET CAFÉ & DONUT EMPORIUM concept is new and untested in Canada, and rapid technology developments may have negative impacts on a Franchisee's business. Further, the Franchisor and its principals have limited experience as an EMMA & JEREMY'S INTERNET CAFÉ & DONUT EMPORIUM Franchisor. As well, although the Franchisor has been advised by the Licensor that the Licensor has had excellent results with the Emma & Jeremy's Internet Café & Donut Emporium System in Bulgaria, and believed use of the Emma & Jeremy's Internet Café & Donut Emporium counselling techniques machine will help to reduce weight as described above, there can be no guarantees that weight will, in fact, be lost among customers. The Franchisor provides no claim that the system will work to reduce weight, although it believes that it will.

Whether the concept went like gangbusters in Bulgaria, Alabama, or Australia does not mean it will go gangbusters in Canada. Think carefully and critically about the concept's successes in foreign markets. Maybe there's no competition in Bulgaria. Maybe land and labour costs are ridiculously low in Alabama. Maybe donuts are the national food of Australia, which explains high sales there. So there may be many reasons why foreign experience should not necessarily be indicative of how well the franchise will perform in Canada. We're a different market, and indeed, each of the provinces can be said to be different markets. Also note the provision, "The Franchisor provides no claim that the system will work to reduce weight, although it believes that it will" merely discloses a belief rather than a fact.

7. FRANCHISEE'S COSTS ASSOCIATED WITH ESTABLISHMENT OF THE FRANCHISE

The franchisor is required to list its estimated costs of establishing the business. There will usually be a "high and low" of these costs. It's up to you to be satisfied as to the accuracy of these costs. If they relate only to the franchisor's experience in Ontario, will those costs be equivalent in BC or Nova Scotia? Where possible, speak to other franchisees as to whether these costs reflect their actual experience. If the franchisor is constructing and developing the premises itself, can you discuss the possibility of a cap on construction costs or a fixed-fee agreement whereby costs do not exceed an agreed upon amount?

Sometimes, one can make numbers say anything. That is why disclosure documents often contain the assumptions underlining the costs that the franchisor has identified. Review the franchisor's assumptions carefully. Do they appear to be inline with your experience? Often, having an accountant review the franchisor's financial statements (attached to the disclosure document) will assist you in making this determination.

Don't forget that some of these numbers will be estimates based on the franchisor's experience. The franchisor may not have any experience in the Canadian market and may be importing its US experience with US costs, which may not be relevant to the Canadian market. Costs set out in the franchisor's US FDD or US-based pro forma financial statements will be in US, not Canadian dollars, and will be based on the franchisor's US experience, not its Canadian one. If they've simply extrapolated US assumptions regarding anticipated Canadian sales (and costs of sales), this may also be unrealistic in a Canadian market one tenth the size of the US market. Import duties might not be included, nor might GST and PST or the costs of packaging and re-labelling products for sale in Canada. Canadians, who tend to have less disposable income and spend more money on tax than Americans, might not be inclined to buy the product or service like Americans might, or the concept may be the next McDonald's.

8. RESTRICTIONS ON SOURCES OF PRODUCTS AND SERVICES

The Franchisor has or will identify various suppliers of Designated Equipment, Products, and/or Services that Franchisees must purchase, lease, use, or provide and that meet EMMA & JEREMY'S INTERNET CAFÉ & DONUT EMPORIUM standards and requirements, in each case as the Franchisor considers appropriate.

The Franchisee must immediately stop selling or using any unapproved items/suppliers.

Will the franchisor consider alternate suppliers of products if the quality is the same as the franchisor's? This may be important when the source of supply of the franchisor's product is interrupted or the cost of obtaining product through the franchisor's supplier is out of line from other suppliers.

9. REBATES AND OTHER BENEFITS TO THE FRANCHISOR

The Franchisor and/or its affiliated companies may derive revenue from the purchase of approved products or services by Franchisees in the form of discounts, volume rebates, payments, commissions, or other concessions that the Franchisor may obtain from any person by reason of its supplying goods to Franchisees and retain for its own account, or share with Franchisees, at its sole option.

The franchisor may retain for its own account rebates it receives from suppliers for volume purchases. This is normal, although some franchisors will roll some or all rebates back into the franchised system to underwrite the advertising fund or other joint operations.

10. FINANCING

The Franchisor does not normally expect to offer direct or indirect financing. Franchisees are directed to make inquiries of a Canadian Chartered Bank or other facility.

11. TRAINING

A training program, which provides technical training on donut cooking, sushi making, and weight-loss counselling is provided to Franchisees by the Franchisor's Licensor. The training is mandatory and must be satisfactorily completed by the Franchisee. Tuition is included in the Training Fee, which is paid by the Franchisee. All Franchisees must pay for and successfully complete the training, which lasts 5 days.

The Franchisee must arrange transportation to the training location and any accommodation if necessary.

Is five days sufficient training for a business such as this? Where is the training location if the rights are acquired from a Delaware company?

12. ADVERTISING AND MARKETING

The Franchisor plans to establish an advertising, publicity, and marketing fund (the "National Marketing Fund" or "Marketing Fund") for advertising, advertising related, marketing, and/or public relations programs, services, and/or materials as the Franchisor deems necessary or appropriate to promote EMMA & JEREMY'S INTERNET CAFÉ & DONUT EMPORIUM Stores and the Brand.

> The Franchisor has sole discretion over all matters relating to the Marketing Fund, operational, marketing, or any other matter (consistent with the Franchise Agreement). The Marketing Fund may be used for (among other things) product development; signage; creation, production, and distribution of marketing, advertising, public relations, and other materials in any medium, including the Internet; administration expenses; brand/image campaigns; media; national, regional, and other marketing programs; activities to promote current and/or future EMMA & JEREMY'S INTERNET CAFÉ & DONUT EMPORIUM stores and the trademark; agency and consulting services; research, any expenses approved by the Franchisor.

It is quite standard for the franchisor to establish an advertising fund in which all franchisees contribute money on a regular basis. The fund is based upon each franchisee's gross sales; the norm being anywhere from 1 to 4 percent of the franchisee's gross sales. It can be a flat fee as well.

The franchisor often supports the fund in the early days of the franchise; it loans the fund money to get the fund up to a level in which meaningful media advertising programs can be undertaken. Naturally, the franchisor is contractually entitled to a return of these loans at some point in time. As well, the franchisor usually provides that it can pay itself a fee for management of the fund and to offset overhead and related charges.

It is important that the franchise agreement contain a provision requiring a yearly accounting of the fund to be undertaken and the statements provided to you and the other franchisees in order that you can see where the advertising dollars have actually been spent and in what media. Is the franchisor permitted to use the fund for advertisements primarily dedicated to selling franchises? I would hope not.

13. OBLIGATION TO PARTICIPATE IN THE ACTUAL OPERATION OF THE FRANCHISE BUSINESS

The EMMA & JEREMY'S INTERNET CAFÉ & DONUT EMPORIUM store must be personally managed on a full-time basis by a person who has successfully completed all training required by the Franchisor and who meets all of our other then-current standards.

This means that absentee management will not be acceptable and that you must not be involved in other businesses that would take you away from the franchise.

14. RENEWAL, TERMINATION, TRANSFER, AND DISPUTE RESOLUTION

The franchisor must list or describe in some detail renewal, termination, transfer, and dispute resolution provisions, which are sometimes displayed in a table. The franchise agreement is the definitive agreement.

15. LICENSES REQUIRED

In Ontario, the franchisor must disclose all licenses and permits that a franchisee must obtain to open the business. If there are special licenses required by you, they should be listed here. An example might be registration under an act that regulates travel agents or direct sellers. Although shoe salesman and donut vendors don't normally require licenses, do sushi chefs? You might need to investigate this.

Remember that an established Canadian franchisor in Ontario with a track record and a number of operating outlets might know exactly what is required, but an out of province franchisor or one from another country might be less familiar with legal requirements to operate the business.

16. EXISTING FRANCHISEE AND FRANCHISOR OUTLETS

The Franchisor has only recently commenced its franchising activities and accordingly has three franchised outlets open in Canada as of the date of this Disclosure Document. See the chart below for details.

Contact the people included in the chart. That's why the regulations require them to be listed. If they're happy, making money, and would do it all again, you probably have a sufficient degree of comfort, even for a ridiculous concept such as this.

Location	Address	Name	Number
Oak Bay, BC	1234 Wiens Avenue, Oak Bay, BC	Natalie Devitt	604-555-1212
Harbour Grace, NF	42 Rompkey Street, Harbour Grace, NF	Hepburn Eng	709-555-1212
Shawnigan Lake, BC	74 Baron Street, Shawnigan Lake, BC	Roger Hearn	604-555-1212

Although not required under CFA disclosure guidelines (or Alberta or Ontario legislation), to assist prospective Franchisees, a list of EMMA & JEREMY'S INTERNET CAFÉ & DONUT EMPORIUM outlets located throughout the world is attached as Schedule "B" hereto.

Franchisees in other parts of the world will likely be franchisees of a different entity (i.e., either a subsidiary or affiliate of the franchisor or perhaps a master franchisee or area franchisor who has obtained its rights from the worldwide franchise company). The foreign list is great information, but may not be of much use to you because you're likely contracting with someone else.

17. FRANCHISE CLOSURE

As of the date of this Disclosure Document, no centres have been terminated, no centres have been denied renewal, or have otherwise closed in the last 3 years in Canada. This is because the concept is so new.

Franchisors are required to disclose the closures of franchise locations or any reasons in the three-year period immediately proceeding the date of the disclosure document. If you are concerned, you should telephone or otherwise contact former franchisees to assess why they left. If the franchisor has no such three-year history, it will not be able to disclose this. All the more reason to contact existing franchisees.

18. EARNINGS CLAIMS AND ESTIMATE OF ANNUAL OPERATING COSTS

The Franchisor makes no earnings claims, and the Franchisor does not give or authorize its salespersons to give any oral or written information concerning the actual or potential sales, cost, income, or profit of a store nor an estimate of annual operating costs. Actual results may vary from franchise to franchise and the Franchisor cannot reasonably estimate the results of any particular franchise.

It is difficult to "sell" ("grant" or "award" is usually what they will call it) a franchise without the franchisor providing some information to you as to how much you will make in this business. This can constitute an earnings claim and requires specific disclosure, in particular the underlining assumptions and the franchisor's basis for making such claims.

19. TRADE-MARKS

Franchisees should understand that there is always a possibility there might be one or more businesses similar to a traditional EMMA & JEREMY'S INTERNET CAFÉ & DONUT EMPORIUM Store operating in or near the area(s) where the Franchisee may do business, and using a name and/or trade-marks similar to EMMA & JEREMY'S INTERNET CAFÉ & DONUT EMPORIUM and with potentially superior rights to the name and/or trade-marks.

Trade-mark information was provided at the beginning of the disclosure document. Remember that the trade-mark in our example is not formally registered. A party other than the franchisor had made application for the mark with the Canadian Intellectual Property Office, but had not yet secured registration of the mark.

The trade-mark process can take anywhere between one and three years. What happens if you have acquired the franchise and commenced using these trade-marks, only to find that the franchisor cannot obtain a registration of these trade-marks? Will you be required by the franchisor to choose other trade-marks and to spend the money required to "re-identify."

20. MEDIATION

Mediation is a voluntary process to resolve disputes with the assistance of an independent third party. Any party may propose mediation or other dispute resolution process in regard to a dispute under the Franchise Agreement, and the process may be used to resolve the dispute if agreed to by all parties.

The Franchisor and Franchisee may invoke the alternative dispute resolution mechanisms of mediation and arbitration at any time, and in respect of any dispute, other than claims relating to the validity of the trade-marks or any intellectual property licensed to the Franchisee, or claims relating to possession of real or personal property, which are the subject of court proceedings pursuant to section 11.7 of the Franchise Agreement. Sections 11.15 and 11.16 contain a comprehensive description of the process and the appointment requirements.

In Ontario, franchise disclosure documents are required to contain this statement. Mediation allows the parties to use the assistance of an impartial "mediator" to attempt to work out a solution between the parties. In successful mediations, the excessive legal fees that can occur in litigation (i.e., going to court) can be significantly reduced or eliminated. You may want to ask if the franchise allows for arbitration of disputes instead of litigation. (Arbitration is the process in which an arbitrator is hired to decide the issue between the parties like a judge as opposed to a mediator, who does not make a decision but who attempts to facilitate a settlement.)

21. TERRITORY

The Franchisor grants the Franchisee a limited license only to operate a single EMMA & JEREMY'S INTERNET CAFÉ & DONUT EMPORIUM outlet using the System (that is, using the trade-marks) at the Franchised Location Premises. The Franchisor does not grant an exclusive territory, but rather agrees that it will not establish and operate, nor grant to any person (other than the Franchisee) the right to establish and operate a centre anywhere within a pre-agreed geographical territory, the borders of which are specified in each Franchise Agreement.

Is the franchisor granting you some form of protected or exclusive territory or protected or exclusive trading area to operate the business? Sometimes the protected trading area granted to you is not real, in the sense that the franchisor agrees not to operate itself or license another entity to operate the same franchise within a five-kilometre radius of your outlet, but will grant you a right of first refusal within that territory to develop another store if the franchisor determines that population and demographics justify another store in that area. If you are unable to exercise the right of first refusal or do not exercise it within the set time period prescribed in the agreement, then the franchisor is entitled to develop the location for itself, or license another party to enter into the territory.

You should be aware of the clause in the franchise agreement that grants the franchisor a reserved right to distribute products or services through "alternative channels of distribution" within your protected territory. Effectively, this means that even though the franchisor may be somehow restricted from operating or licensing or franchising a store within your protected territory, the franchisor is not barred from selling the product that is normally sold by you to retail department or food stores for inevitable sale to the public.

22. NOTICE OF RESCISSION AND EFFECT OF CANCELLATION (ALBERTA)

Alberta law requires franchisors to repeat certain sections of the Alberta statute dealing with remedies. Check with a franchise lawyer for more information.

Ontario has similar, though not identical remedies under its laws in the event the franchisor has breached the act.

23. FINANCIAL STATEMENTS

The Financial Statements of the Franchisor dated February 5, 2004, are attached as Schedule "C".

Franchisors are required to attach their most recent financial statements for their most recent completed year to the disclosure document. In Alberta and Ontario, these may be audited financial statements or they may be done on a review engagement basis by an accountant. In either case, the audit or review must be performed by an independent accountant. You may consider having your accountant briefly examine these statements. Start-up franchisors sometimes have no financial year and are permitted to attach an opening balance sheet.

CERTIFICATE

Unless the franchisor has one shareholder and one director, at least two representatives of the franchisor must certify the accuracy of the disclosure document. Not only must they certify that all material facts required by the act have been disclosed, but that they have not omitted a material fact that might affect your decision to make the investment. As it is a certification as to accuracy, it has to be signed to be effective. The certification provisions under each of the statutes are different.

Attached to the disclosure document should be the financial statements of the franchisor as well as all the agreements the franchisor uses with its franchisees.

GLOSSARY

Co-terminus: One agreement runs together with another agreement, such as a franchise agreement and a sublease starting and ending on the same day.

Cross default: A cross default clause essentially provides that a default under one agreement with the franchisor is a default under all agreements with the franchisor.

Curable default: A default under an agreement that is usually "fixable" on 7, 14, or 30 days (or however long the franchisor prescribes). It could be a monetary default, curable by the payment of money, or it could be an operational default such as staff not wearing the correct uniforms. These defaults can be cured, if the agreement allows for curing.

Disclosure document: A document mandated by the laws of Ontario and Alberta (and also under the rules of the Canadian Franchise Association), whereby franchisors are required to disclose to a prospective franchisee (before franchise agreements are entered or non-refundable monies paid) all material facts relating to the franchisor and the franchise system. (Material facts being facts that might influence a prospective franchisee to acquire or not acquire the franchise had he or she known of such facts.)

Electronic funds transfer: Automatic transfer of funds from the bank account of the franchisee to that of the franchisor.

Gross sales: All sales generated from the franchised business, with a deduction for GST, PST, and bona fide returns. Royalties are normally based on a percentage of the gross sales made by the franchisee.

Guarantor: A person or company that agrees to pay someone else's debt or perform someone else's obligation in the event that such person or company can't or won't pay the debt or perform the obligation.

Head lease: A lease entered by a franchisor or other party that allows (or contemplates) that the lease will be sublet to a franchisee. Whereas most leases won't allow the tenant to sublet without the landlord's express consent, a head lease will allow subletting to a franchisee without the landlord's express consent (as the franchisor is ultimately responsible under the head lease for performance under the lease).

Master franchisee: Sometimes called an area franchisor and sometimes called a master franchisor. (The terms master franchisor and master franchisee are unfortunately used interchangeably, depending on the lawyer.) Here, we are calling a franchisee with a territory and the right to enter franchise agreements with franchisees (called sub franchisees or unit franchisees) and the right to open up a stores in that territory on its own account a "master franchisee."

Non-competition clause: A covenant that legally precludes a party from competing with another party for an agreed period of time and within an agreed area. Courts are reluctant to enforce restrictive covenants as they deem them restraints of trade. They are only enforceable if they are "reasonable."

Non-curable defaults: These defaults are impossible (or at least very difficult) to cure and normally include things such as a franchisee's bankruptcy; insolvency; the appointment of a receiver; the franchisee abandoning the business; the franchisee selling the business without the franchisor's consent; or the franchisee taking down the signs and calling itself something else.

Pro forma financial statements: Estimated financial statements based upon a projection of performance in the future rather than actual performance from the past.

Restrictive covenant: Essentially the same as a non-competition clause.

Royalties: An ongoing payment for the use of the franchisor's business system and trade-mark, as well as the franchisor's support under a franchise agreement. Normally expressed as a percentage of gross sale.

Tripartite agreements: Agreements between three parties. In the franchise industry, normally an agreement between the franchisor, the franchisee, and a landlord giving the franchisor rights to take back premises or cure a franchisee's default. Landlords are more likely to want a direct agreement from the franchisor in the event the franchisee is terminated rather than negotiating these tripartite agreements.

Withholding taxes: Taxes required to be paid on royalties that are payable outside Canada. There are no withholding taxes payable on royalties paid by a Canadian franchisee to a Canadian franchisor. There are withholding taxes payable on royalties paid by a Canadian franchisee to a US franchisor in the US (although if the US franchisor has created a Canadian subsidiary to collect royalties from Canadian franchisees, no withholding taxes are payable).